A Brief Narrative of the Historical and Geographic Attributes of the Uyghur Identity

---- *And Its Substantial Difference from the Turkic Identity and the Turkish Identity*

Mark Chuanhang Shan

MarkChuanhangShan@gmail.com

Translated from Chinese by Charlene L. Fu

*This booklet is dedicated
to the Uyghur and Han Chinese friends in my hometown,
Xinjiang, China*

A Brief Narrative of the Historical and Geographic Attributes of the Uyghur Identity
---- And Its Substantial Difference from the Turkic Identity and the Turkish Identity

November sixth, 2018 published by Chinese Christian Theological Association
874 Beacon Street, Boston, Massachusetts, 02215- 3101USA
www.CCTA.me
© 2018 by Mark Chuanhang Shan
All rights reserved. No part of this book may be reproduced in any form without permission from the author.
ISBN-13: 978-0578415598   ISBN-10: 0578415593
Printed in the United States of America

Table of Contents

A note from the author ……….. 1

Note on Transliteration, People and Place Names, and other Scholarly Conventions ……….. 7

Foreword ……….. 10

Introduction ……….. 11

I. The Historical and Geographic Attributes of the Uyghur Identity ……….. 14

   1. Proto-Uyghurs before AD 744: the historical emergence of the Uyghurs on the East Asian steppes ……….. 15

   2. Examining and rectifying extant historical narratives: Clarifying the different ethnic attributes of the "Uyghur" and the "Turk", differentiating Uyghurization and Turkification ……….. 36

   3. The rise and fall of the Uyghurs in East Asia: the Orkhon Khanate Uyghurs (744-848) ……….. 69

   4. The Independent Kocho Khanate Uyghurs (841–1130): the origin of Uyghuristan and the modern Uyghur identity ……….84

II. Clarifying the Difference between the Uyghurs and the People of Turkey ………… 101

    1. The origins and formation of Turkey ………… 104

    2. Clarifying the ethnic attributes in the historical names for the Hunnic-Turkic speaking people of Central Asia: Oghuz, Ghuzz, Toquz Oghuz and Toquz Uyghur ………… 115

    3. The pre-1949 struggles of the Uyghur people on identity restoration ………… 129

Epilogue ………… 147

By Mark C. H. Shan 2018

A Brief Narrative of the Historical and Geographic Attributes of the Uyghur Identity

---- And Its Substantial Difference from the Turkic Identity and the Turkish Identity

By Mark Chuanhang Shan

Translated from Chinese by Charlene L. Fu

A note from the author

This paper is a slightly modified excerpt from chapters one and two of my PhD thesis: *The Historical Uyghur Identity and its Attributes from Kocho Civilization and East-Syriac Christianity*, submitted on July 31, 2018 in the English version. By adopting a historical anthropology framework, through an approach of a history discipline coupled with religious studies and engaging carefully in textual analysis of the original historical records, the thesis uses **the five-dimensional attributes system of geography, history, ethnicity, religion and civilization.** These attributes were created and developed for the purpose of constructing an identity narrative to explore the historical changes and transformation of the Uyghur ethnic identity, with the hope of offering to the

A Brief Narrative of the Historical and Geographic Attributes of the Uyghur Identity

Uyghurs who live in Xinjiang, China an alternative narrative of their identity.

A common narrative exists in academia that the Uyghurs, after migrating from the Mongol steppes to Xinjiang and becoming the Kocho Uyghurs, initially remained Manicheans, then became Buddhists, with Christianity as only a minority religion among them. This thesis clarifies that the Kocho Uyghurs were mostly Christians converted from Manichaeism after a time, but were never officially Buddhists, with only a handful of Uyghurs actually accepting Buddhism. In addition, Uyghur Manichaeism did not disappear, but continued to exist in a highly mutated form through a concealed way. The reasons for this easily made misunderstanding by scholars are also clarified in this paper. Therefore, the religious attribute of the Uyghurs' Kocho civilization was primarily East Syriac Christianity, though the Manichean attribute was also present in its earlier transitional stage. This is the answer to the commonly recognized historical puzzle of why the Uyghurs and some other Turkic speaking kingdoms in Central-East Asia were suddenly known as being strongly Christian nations after their conquest by the Chenghis Khan's Mongols, so much so that their Uyghur civilization, with its Christian attributes, even transformed the Mongol Empire among the Mongol royal families.

Through a very long process of changes to the five-dimensional attributes of the Uyghur identity, only the Uyghurs living in Xinjiang today who are Islamified and seemingly Turkified are regarded as Uyghurs, and only the Beiting (Urumqi) and Kocho (Turpan) Uyghurs are the symbolic and comparatively pure-blood descendants of the Uyghurs of the period from 755 to 1392. From the perspective of the historical anthropology of religion and ethnicity, this historic process of identity change and transformation can be understood as progressing through the following **five major religious-ethnic stages**: Shamanist grassland Uyghur, Manichaean Orkhon Uyghur, Christian Kocho Uyghur, Islamic Chagatai Uyghur, and Islamic Xinjiang Uyghur. Of these five stages, the Christian Kocho (Turpan) Uyghur identity represents the Kocho civilization that civilized the Mongol Empire, reaching the historic peak of Uyghurish civilization.

Another universally accepted yet misleading narrative insists that Uyghurs are Turks or Turkic. The Uyghurs, according to the Chinese classics, were originally of the Tlugh (*Tie-le* or *Te-le*) ethnic group of the East Asian Steppes, which in turn was descended from the Huns (*Xiong-nu*), and later congregated at the Selenge-Orkhon-Tuul rivers region. The Uyghurs are not, as people have long believed, Turks (or Turki), although their language is classified by linguists as a Turkic language. Turks, according to the Chinese classics, were originally of the mixed blood *Hu* people from the He-xi Corridor (Gan-su region) and later congregated at the Altai Mountains. They were likely related to the *Gao-che* Indo-Europeans of East and North Asia. In fact, not only are the Uyghurs and the Turks two different ethnic groups, but when they lived on the Mongolian grasslands in ancient times, they were also long-time enemies. The history of the Turks is shorter than that of the Uyghurs.

The identity of the Turks as the Hunnified "mixed-blood *Hu*" evolved significantly through history as a result of large-scale and long-term westward migrations and intermixing with the native Indo-Europeans of Central Asia that they colonized. Through this, Turkic civilizations remained prevalent through the Turkification of others, and ultimately was imposed by the dominant Islamic tribute. Thus, the Turks were Islamified. The symbolic descendants of Turks today are Turkic Turkoman who later intermixed with their conquerors the Chenghis Mongols and their more mutated kinsmen, the Turkish people of Turkey living to the far west, who heavily intermixed with the Armenian and Greeks that they ruled over.

The identity of the Uyghurs as the authentic Hunnic descendants evolved throughout history because of migration and intermixing with the native Indo-Europeans of the Tarim basin that they colonized. Their civilizations were not ultimately successful in resisting Turkic-Mongol

Islamification. Today, they live in the Xinjiang Uyghur Autonomous Region of northwest China, while their slightly mutated kinsmen, the Uzbeks, are living on the other side of the Pamir Mountains to the west. The Uyghurs are identified as a people who are uniformly Muslim. Xinjiang, at the eastern edge of Central Asia, has since ancient times been a region where many nationalities and civilizations have converged and collided. As the site of the Silk Road's major thoroughfare, this region has been repeatedly fought over by various ethnic groups and kingdoms around the regions along the Silk Road.

Since 1759, Xinjiang has been a part of China, after being acquired through warfare by the Manchu Qing government. Today, the Uyghur population in Xinjiang stands at approximately 10 million according to the provincial government, followed by approximately 9 million Han-Chinese. The remaining population consists of approximately two million people of other Turkic speaking and non-Turkic speaking ethnic groups, most of whom believe in Islam.

Xinjiang's present population is more than 21,586,300, according to the Xinjiang government's late 2009 census.[1] That's approximately a five-fold increase from the 1949 population of 4,333,400, and almost double

---

[1] Jin Jianxin (ed.), Statistics Bureau of Xinjiang Uyghur Autonomous Region, *Xinjiang Statistical Yearbook 2010* (Urumqi, China Statistics Press, 2010), 77. (《新疆统计年鉴-2010》)

the 1976 population of 11,858,000. In 1949, the non-Han population stood at 4,042,400 or 93% of the total population, in 1976, non-Hans numbered 6,949,100, or 59%.[2] By 2010, Xinjiang had a total of 47 nationalities, of which 13 are major ones. The Uyghur population is 10,019,758; Han 8,416,867; Kazakh 1,514,814; Hui (Tongan) 980,359; Kyrgyz 189,309; Mongol 179,615; Tajik 47,187; Xibe (Sibo) 42,790; Manchu 26,195; Uzbek 16,669; Russian 11,672; Daur 6,992; Tatar 4,883; and other ethnic groups 129,190.[3] Among these 47 nationalities, the Uyghurs and the Han Chinese, the two largest nationalities, account for 46.42% and 38.99% of Xinjiang's population, respectively.

Mark Chuanhang Shan

November 06, 2018, Boston, USA

---

[2] This is based on internal materials and information from statistics offices of the Xinjiang government.

[3] Jin, *Yearbook 2010*, 92; Li, *Xinjiang*, Foreword, 5-6.

Note on Transliteration, People and Place Names, and other Scholarly Conventions

Because so many place names, names of people, and other names and terms that originate from different languages, including Uyghur, Chinese, Mongolian, Persian, Syriac, and Arabic, appear in this thesis, and because different names and terms are sometimes used in different languages and different periods for the same thing, some scholarly conventions need to be established to standardize the handling of these many different names and terms.

1. Except where an accepted English name and spelling already exists, the transliteration of all non-English names is italicized, and they are spelled using the English alphabet. For Turkic language transliteration, the letter "k" and "q" will be used interchangeably. Regarding the term Khan, the newer spelling is Qaghan, but the former will be used to honor those scholars who laid the foundation for Xinjiang and Uyghur studies in the early 20th century.

2. The Chinese names for modern people, places, and other designations are not italicized and are rendered in standard Pinyin, without tone marks. Modern refers to the period after the start of World War I, that is, after 1914.

3. The names of people, places, and other designations in ancient Chinese are rendered in standard Pinyin without tone marks. The transliteration of the characters of a person's name in ancient Chinese are separated by a hyphen and are not italicized. Place names, ethnic names, and other designations are italicized (except those that are in quotation marks) and if necessary, also with a hyphen. Ancient refers to pre-World War I, that is, before 1914.

4. Because the name "Xinjiang" has since 1759 referred specifically to a province or provincial-level administrative region of China, the use of "Xinjiang", "the Xinjiang area" or "the Xinjiang region" to refer to this geographic location prior to 1759 refers to the roughly corresponding area of ancient times and is not meant to highlight the provincial nature of the term. In this usage, the borders of this area are inexact. Furthermore, North Xinjiang refers to the area in Xinjiang that is north of the Tianshan mountain range, while South Xinjiang refers to the area south of the Tianshan mountain range. East Xinjiang refers to the area surrounding the tail end of the easternmost part of the Tianshan mountain range, adjacent to present-day Gansu and Qinghai provinces. The use of these names is for ease of expression and helps readers gain a clear sense of geographic orientation.

5. When possible to do so without affecting the clarity of the thesis, the name "Xinjiang" will be sparingly

used. In its stead, use will sometimes be made of "Western Regions" or "*An-xi*" (that is, Chinese Protectorate General to Pacify the West), or geographic terms such as mountain range, basin, river, or lake. The use of Western Regions or *An-xi* is necessitated by the fact that these are the names used in ancient Chinese historical sources, a core reference resource of this thesis.

These conventions, hopefully, resolve some of the confusion and frustration that scholars of Xinjiang and Central Asia have long encountered in their research.

A Brief Narrative of the Historical and Geographic Attributes of the Uyghur Identity and Its Substantial Difference from the Turkic Identity and the Turkish Identity

By Mark Chuanhang Shan

Translated from Chinese by Charlene L. Fu

Foreword

To take on an identity is actually a process of attaching meaning to that identity; therefore, it is not a static definition nor a perpetual agreement, but rather a pursuit of growth in one's cognitive awareness of oneself and of one's group, community or nation. In the pursuit of a sense of identity, when the bonds within one collective identity grow stronger, discrimination of groups with different identities will also intensify.

Therefore, to construct an ideal sense of identity, people are prone to creating selective historical narratives, geographic descriptions and ethnic background accounts, to the point of avoiding or even sacrificing some truths when in the midst of an identity crisis or for beneficial gains. Regardless of whether it is the individual, the family, the ethnic group, the race, the nation, or any other community of shared interests, all will choose selectively to some degree or other. Even mankind as a whole has trouble reaching a consensus on its own sense of original identity. For example, evolutionism and creationism both seek to control the definition of mankind's identity through a worldview and a historical view. Within the framework of understanding this kind of meaning, neither the disadvantaged group that is the subject of this thesis, the Xinjiang Uyghurs, nor the dominant Han Chinese are exceptions.

Introduction

Today, most Uyghurs live within China's borders, in the Xinjiang Uyghur Autonomous Region (a provincial-level administrative region), in northwestern China. Currently the two largest ethnic groups in Xinjiang are the Uyghurs and the ruling ethnic group of the Han Chinese, together accounting for about 85 percent of the population (21.58 million). Most of the remaining 15 percent of Xinjiang's population belong to other Turkic speaking and non-Turkic speaking ethnic groups. Visitors to Xinjiang quickly realize that not only are the language and customs of the Uyghurs and the Han Chinese vastly different, but their facial features are also distinctly different. Even amongst the Uyghurs themselves, there are surprising and puzzling differences in facial features.

A Brief Narrative of the Historical and Geographic Attributes of the Uyghur Identity

In ancient times, the Uyghur people were the outstanding representatives of the Turkic language speaking ethnic groups. Originally from the Mongolian steppes, their forefathers—whom the Romans called "Huns" and the Chinese called *Xiong-nu* (*Hsiung-nu*)—were the nomadic military forces that were a severe trial for both the Han Chinese and later the ancient Romans. For more than one thousand years, since 841, the Uyghur people have lived in the territory that is present-day Xinjiang of China, but for most of that time after 1130 and up to present-day, they were ruled by other ethnic groups. Because the earlier indigenous people of Xinjiang were Indo-European whites, whose numbers are few today, and because their descendants are of mixed blood due to intermixing with Uyghurs and others, misunderstandings exist about the historical, geographic, and ethnic attributes of the Uyghurs.

This paper uses a historical anthropology framework, dominated by historical methodology, through textual analysis of mostly Chinese classics and Turkic language inscriptions, to abstract the historical and geographic attributes of the identity of Xinjiang Uyghurs, and to clarify that they are neither Turkic nor Turkish people. The research will help people understand Uyghurs and their struggles and attempts to characterize an operable identity today in their politically and religiously turbulent world.

The first part of this paper will explore the historical attributes and geographic attributes of the Uyghur people, with clarification of the fact that Uyghurs are not Turks, so they are not of the Turkic groups. The historical attributes will include consideration of where the Uyghur people originated, the history of their ethnic development, and the history of their relationship with other ethnic groups. The geographic attributes will be mainly the Mongolian steppes, the birthplace of the Hunnic-Uyghur people, and present-day Xinjiang, the land to which they migrated. Xinjiang is the most important of the geographic coordinates; it is deeply ingrained in the Uyghur consciousness, and hence a detailed discussion and clarification (which is not included in this excerpt but in the thesis) is needed of the history of the Xinjiang region and its ethnic histories so as to help restore to the Uyghur people their unique fact-based identity.

The second part of this paper will explore and clarify the fact that Uyghurs are not people of Turkey and thus they are not of the Turkish group. It also clarifies the complexity regarding the ethnic attributes in the historical names for the Turkic speaking groups of Central Asia, which have misled and confused people and scholars for too long. Finally, it analyzes the pre-1949 struggles of the Uyghurs for their ethnic identity restoration with rediscovering their long-lost ethnic name, "Uyghur", as a significant though very short-lived cultural and political victory, and their identity crisis under the rule of the Han Chinese government.

This paper carefully uses these terms with their different designated meanings: Uyghur, Uyghurish,[4] and Uyghur language; Tlugh, Tlughur and Tlughish;[5] Turk (Turki), Turkic and Turkic language; Turkey, Turkish and Turkish language; and even Uyghur speaking, Tlughish speaking, Turkic speaking and Turkish speaking. All of these groups and their languages can be traced back to the ancient Hunnic root either ethnically or culturally.

I. The Historical and Geographic Attributes of the Uyghur Identity

The historical and geographic attributes of the Uyghur identity went through four major stages: 1) proto-Uyghurs (before AD 744), 2) Orkhon Khanate Uyghurs (744-841), 3) migrated Uyghurs (841-866), and 4) Kocho Uyghurs (841-1130). Migrated Uyghurs consisted of two branches, southward and westward branches, with the latter dividing into three sub-groups: the Hexi Corridor

---

[4] "Uyghurish" is the term that I have developed to be used as an adjective to conveniently distinguish from "Turkic" and "Turkish".

[5] These three terms have also been created by me to designate the ethnic group including Uyghurs, Kazakhs, and others, and to distinguish from the Turkic group including Turks, Ghuzz, and others.

Uyghurs, the Kocho Uyghurs, and the Kara-Khannid Uyghurs. Of all the Uyghur groups, only the Kocho Uyghurs living in the region of the eastern Tianshan mountain range were the ones who preserved their Uyghur identity for the longest. They are the ones who became the symbolic forefathers of the comparatively pure-blooded Uyghurs of present-day Xinjiang.

1. Proto-Uyghurs before AD 744: the historical emergence of the Uyghurs on the East Asian steppes

The Uyghurs are descendents of what the ancient Chinese called the *Xiong-nu* people. Ancient Chinese historians documented the lives of the *Xiong-nu,* long a troublesome neighbor, and their history can be traced back to as early as 1200 BC. In non-Chinese historical records, the Romans and Indians called the *Xiong-nu* "Huns", or also "Hunni" or "Huna",[6] all likely derived from the transliteration of the same name. Later, they were also called *"Tie-le"* or *"Te-le"* from ancient Chinese transliteration. Uyghurs at that time were part of *"Tie-le"* or *"Te-le"*. The ancestral home of the Uyghurs was not present-day Xinjiang but rather the East Asian steppes, better known as the Mongolian grasslands.

---

[6] René Grousset, *The Empire of the Steppes: A History of Central Asia*, Naomi Walford (tr.), (New Brunswick: Rutgers University Press, 2002), 19.

It is commonly agreed that the earliest records with great details of the Huns are in ancient Chinese-language historical sources. There are also great details about the *Tie-le* or *Te-le* groups, as well as the Turks and Uyghurs as they were all immediate neighbors and threats to the Chinese to the south. The first European encounter with the Huns was in the 4th century. Similar to the negative comments of Han dynasty China historians Si-ma Qian and Ban Gu in the second century BC, Roman historian Ammianus Marcellinus in the 4th century called the barbaric Huns "ugly beasts" and a "wild race".[7] In the first half of the 5th century, Huns, especially those led by Attila the Hun who established a Hunnic kingdom in Europe and had defeated the Roman Empire several times,[8] contributed to the fall of the Western Roman Empire. From the ancient Chinese-language records, it is clear that the nomadic Huns had posed a grave threat to China from the north and fought constantly with the sedentary Han Chinese. The Hun ethnic group included different sub-groups, each with slight differences.

The 10th century Chinese historical record *Old Book of Tang* (***OBoT***[9]) clearly explains the origins of the

---

[7] Walter Hamilton (tr.), *Ammianus Marcellinus: The Later Roman Empire (354-378)* (London: Penguin Classics, 2004), 411-412.

[8] Arnold Hugh Martin Jones, *The Later Roman Empire 284-602* (Oxford: Basil Blackwell, 1964), 193-94.

[9] This thesis uses the abbreviations *OBoT* and *NBoT* to refer to the *Old Book of Tang* and *New Book of Tang*, respectively.

Uyghur ethnic identity: their ancestors were the Huns (*Xiong-nu*), later the *Tie-le* and *Te-le*. They were originally from the Mongolian steppes, but in 841, after the destruction of their kingdom, most of them formally went into exile and many resettled in Xinjiang.[10] The following can essentially be proven by putting together the information from ancient Chinese historical sources: the earliest Huns originated from Northeast Asia, that is, the region of the Greater Khingan Range, the Ussuri River and the lower Amur River (*Hei-long-jiang* River), just as the later groups who like them were of Northeast Asian ethnicity—the *Rou-ran*, the Khitans, the *Jin* (Jurchens), the Mongols, and Manchus—all originated from this same area. In other words, none of these ethnic groups were the earliest inhabitants of the Mongolian steppes which were the paradise of those nomadic native white people.

In ancient Chinese materials, the steppes north of the Yellow River were called Xia, or Central *Xia* (*Zhong Xia*) which refers to non-Chinese people, most likely white people and their territory in its original meaning, corresponding to south of the Yellow River called *Hua*, or Central *Hua* (*Zhong Hua*) which refers to proper China and its Chinese. The meaning of the combination *Hua Xia*, which the Chinese and Chinese governments often use, will be discussed in a later section.

---

[10] Liu Xu, *Old Book of Tang* (*Jiu-tang-shu*, AD 945), Chronicle 145, "Uyghurs (*Hui-he*)" (Beijing: Zhonghua Book Company, 2000), 3535, 3547.（刘昫：《旧唐书》）

The pronunciation of the name "Uyghur" in the Uyghur language is approximately *"wei gu er"*, *"wei hu er"* or *"wei wu er"* to a Chinese ear, and today it means "unity" or "solidarity"; the original meaning was "to join together and help". [11] In China's historical records, Uyghurs and their ancestors were called by various names in Chinese. In the Chinese historical records of various dynasties, they were called *Xian-yun* in the Zhou dynasty (1046-256 BC), *Xiong-nu* in the Han dynasty (206 BC-AD 220), *Tie-le* in the Wei dynasty (386-550), and *Te-le* in the Sui dynasty (581-619); the use of the name Uyghur began in the Tang dynasty (618-907) when it was rendered as *Hui-he* and *Hui-gu*, and as *Wei-wu* and *Wei-wu-er* in the Mongol Empire era (1206-1250). There are a dozen different transliteratons. Beginning in 1450, that is, at the height of the forcible imposition in Xinjiang of Islam by the Mongolian Eastern Chagatai Khanate, the use of the name "Uyghur" ceased for nearly 500 years. [12]

It was not until the 1920s that usage of the ethnonym "Uyghur" resumed, first in 1921 at the Soviet Communist-sponsored meeting in the Uzbek capital of Tashkent, [13] followed in 1925 in the publications in Zhetysu

---

[11] Wheeler M. Thackston (tr.), *Rashiduddin Fazlullah's Compendium of Chronicles* (Cambridge: Harvard University, 1998), 74.

[12] Justin Jon Rudelson, *Oasis Identities: Uygur Nationalism Along China's Silk Road* (New York: Columbia University Press, 1997), 5.

[13] James A Millward, *Eurasian Crossroads: A History of Xinjiang* (New York: Columbia University Press, 2007), 208.

(Semireche in the Soviet Union, *Qi-he* or Seven Rivers region in Chinese) and Moscow.[14] It was not until 1934[15] through the efforts of some modernized Uyghur intellectuals, under the Soviet-influenced Chinese provincial government of Sheng Shicai, that the use of the name "Uyghur" was officially resumed in Xinjiang to differentiate the Uyghurs from other Turkic-speaking ethnic groups.[16] Before this time, the Uyghur people were generally referred to in English with the understandable misnomer of "Turks" to distinguish them from the Kazakhs, the Kyrgyzs, and other ethnic groups, while the Han Chinese called the Uyghurs "Turbaned Head" (*Chantou,* means "wrapped head").[17] The Uyghurs called themselves "Turk" (Türk) or "Turki" (Türki),[18] "Muslim", or names derived from specific locales,[19] such as Kashgaris (Altishahri Uyghur), Taranchis (Jungharian Uyghur),[20] or Turpanese[21] (Kocho Uyghur).

---

[14] David John Brophy, *Uyghur Nation: Reform and Revolution on the Russia-China Frontier* (Cambridge: Harvard University Press, 2016), 220, 222.

[15] Justin Jon Rudelson, *Oasis Identities: Uygur Nationalism Along China's Silk Road* (New York: Columbia University Press, 1997), 7, 149.

[16] Millward, *Crossroads*, 208; Rudelson, *Oasis Identities*, 149.

[17] Millward, *Crossroads*, 208.

[18] Millward, *Crossroads*, 209.

[19] Brophy, *Uyghur Nation*, 141.

[20] Brophy, *Uyghur Nation*, 179, 199.

To date, the earliest records of the Huns are found in 1200 BC oracle bones from late in China's Shang dynasty which referred to this ethnic group as the *Ya-xiong* using the same *xiong* character as in *Xiong-nu*. One scholar states that this name is a transliteration,[22] a view with which I agree. The *Book of Wei*, a history of the Northern Wei compiled from 551 to 554, says: "According to [earlier] court historians, *Xian-yun* in the Zhou dynasty was later *Xiong-nu* in the Han dynasty, and they have long inflicted great harm on China."[23] *Xian-yun* here is similar in today's pronunciation to *Ya-xiong*. In the Chinese classical history books, foreign names were typically handled using transliteration, and were occasionally accompanied by an explanation in Chinese characters of the meaning.

Then, in the late Zhou dynasty and Spring-Autumn period of China, Confucius compiled and edited some Chinese classics, including *Spring and Autumn Annals*

---

[21] I have come up with this new term to recognize the Turpan-Urumqi-Hami Uyghurs as descendents of the ancient Kocho Khanate Uyghurs.

[22] Fang Hanwen, "The Westward Migration of the Huns and the Collapse of Roman Empire", *Root Exploration*, No. 6 of 62 (Henan, China, 2004), 16-23, 17. (方汉文：《匈族(Huns)西迁与罗马帝国的崩溃》)

[23] Wei Shou, *Book of Wei (Wei-Shu* 551-554*)*, Chronicle 91, *Ru-ru, Xiong-nu* (*Huns*), etc. (Beijing: Zhonghua Book Company, 2000), 1565. "史臣曰：周之猃狁，汉之匈奴，其作害中国固亦久矣。" (魏收：《魏书》)

(*Chun-qiu*) which mentioned that some non-Chinese enemies called *Bei-di*,[24] referring to northern *Di* people, were at the time in the northern part of present-day China and in the southern part of the present-day Mongolian grasslands. It also mentions "di", "white di", "red di", and "tall di" (*Chang-di*).[25] These nomadic Di people from the north often attacked Southern China during the final years of the Chinese Zhou Dynasty. They fought those Chinese states for a long time and experienced both victories and defeats. The small Chinese states were mostly located in the present-day Shanxi province, which was the Jin state. The Shannxi province was the Zheng state; north of the Henana province and south of the Hebei province was the Wei state; the current Shandong province was the Qi state and Lu state, etc. *Commentary on Spring and Autumn Annals* (Chun-qiu Zuo-zhuan) has over 170 recordings about the Di people and their battles with the Chinese. *The Classic of Mountains and Seas* (Shan-hai-jing), another classic probably written in the early years of the Warring States through the early years of the Western Han

---

[24] Zuo Qiuming, *Commentary on Spring and Autumn Annals* (*Chun-qiu Zuo-zhuan Zheng-yi,* the 5th century BC), "Duke Xiang (Xianggong)" (Beijing: Peking University Press, 1999), 1045. (《春秋左转正义·襄公》) [李学勤主编：《十三经注疏·春秋左传正义（上、中、下）》]

[25] Zuo Qiuming, *Commentary on Spring and Autumn Annals*, 470, 476, 535-536, 601, 613, 948,1072,1113-1114. (《春秋左转正义》)

dynasty, also mentioned *Bei-di*.[26] Later Chinese historical texts continued using these terms especially "red di" and "white di".

Some even later Chinese historical texts considered these people to be the ancestors of the Hun, but I hold a different view, which is that they were white people living north of Hun. That's because the color component of the names very likely corresponded to skin color. Later in this chapter, a detailed examination will be made of the European-type race, including the ruddy-complexioned Mediterranean type and the pale Aryan type. Although called "European type", these white people had not migrated from Europe but were natives of Xinjiang-Central Asia and the area north of the Yellow River and later of the Great Wall, later called the Mongolian grasslands where they had lived since around 1800 BC. They are first called Indo-Europeans by western philologists in the 18th century,[27] which includes what this thesis calls ruddy-faced Scythian type and pale-faced Tocharain type.

---

[26] Zhou Mingchu (ed.), *The Classic of Mountains and Seas (Shan-hai-jing)*, "Great Western Wilderness" (Hangzhou: Zhejiang Ancient Books Publishing House, 2002), 223. It says: "There is the Kingdom of *Bei-di*. The grandson of the Yellow Emperor is named Shi-jun. Shi-jun is the father of the *Bei-di*." "有北狄之国。皇帝之孙曰始均，始均生北狄。"（《山海经·大荒西经》）

[27] J. P. Mallory and Victor H. Mair, *The Tarim Mummies: Ancient China and the Mystery of the Earliest Peoples from the West* (London, New York: Thames & Hudson Ltd, 2000), 119.

The *Spring and Autumn Annals with the Commentary of Zuo: Yin-gong* reports that in the late Zhou dynasty and in the Spring and Autumn Period, another foreign barbarian enemy, the *Bei-rong*, had attacked several small Han Chinese states to its south (where the first sections of the Great Wall were later built), saying, "The northern *Rong* raided *Zheng*. The earl withstood them... His son Tu said, '... The *Rong* are light and nimble, but have no order; they are greedy and have no love for one another; when they conquer, no one will yield place to his fellow; and when they are defeated, no one tries to save another.'"[28] This description shows that the *Bei-rong* were a savage nomadic people. Note that the *Bei-rong* were likely a sub-group of the Huns, as the pronunciation of *rong* (in *Bei-rong*) and *xiong* (in *Xiong-nu*) are similar. *Bei* refers to the north of China.

The famous Han China historian Ban Gu (AD32-92) provides evidence in his great work *Book of Han* that the ancestors of the Huns in the Yao and Shun eras were also called *Rong*. One passage traces the earliest history of the Huns and the changes in their name: "*Xiong-nu* is the descendant of *Xia*, also called *Chun-wei*. Above *Tang-yu* there were the *Shan-rong*, the *Xian-yun* and the *Xun-yu*,

---

[28] Li Xueqin (ed.), *Chun Qiu Zuo Zhuan from the Complied Commentaries of the Thirteen Classics*, "Dutch Yin", 117.李学勤（主编）：《十三经注疏·春秋左传正义》，"隐公九年"。 "北戎侵郑，郑伯御之。患戎师……公子突曰：……戎轻而不整，贪而无亲，胜不相让，败不相救。……十一月，甲寅，郑人大败戎师。"

who live in the north and migrate with their livestock, following the grass."²⁹ "*Tang-yu*" was a general term used in ancient times to refer to China's earliest territories. "*Shan*", which means mountain, indicates that these *Rong* people lived in the mountains on the steppes, likely including the Taihang Mountains, which at the time were China's northern border region. It is evident from another passage in the same book that these savage nomadic people had been invading China without break since the Shang dynasty (about 1600-1046 BC) and bringing the ravages of war to ordinary people: "*Rong* and *Di* invade by turn, violently oppressing China. China is suffering because of them,…"³⁰ A distinction is made here between *Rong* and *Di*, with *Rong* referring to the ancestors of the Huns, and *Di* being another ethnic group (as will be explained later in this chapter, these were a non-East Asian people, but white people); both were savage nomadic peoples who loved to launch lengthy invasions against the sedentary Chinese to their south.

According to the records of Ban Gu and in *Records of*

---

[29] Ban Gu, *Book of Han* (*Han-shu*, begun by Ban Biao, continued by his son Ban Gu, then by Ban Gu's younger sister Ban Zhao assisted by the historian Ma Xu, and finished around AD 111) Chronicle 64 I, "Xiong-nu [Huns]"(Beijing: Zhonghua Book Company, 2000), 2771. "匈奴，其先夏后氏之苗裔，曰淳维。唐虞以上有山戎、猃狁、薰粥，居于北边，随草畜牧而转移。"(班固：《汉书》)

[30] Ban Gu, *Book of Han*, 2772. "至穆王之孙懿王时，王室遂衰，戎狄交侵，暴虐中国。中国被其苦，……"

the Grand Historian by Si-ma Qian (d. 86 BC),[31] during the Warring States Period, the State of Zhao, situated in the area of present-day Shanxi and Hebei provinces, was successful for a time in resisting the Huns' incursions across its borders and constructed part of the Great Wall. The State of Qin also came under unendurable harassment and built another portion of the Great Wall in the area of present-day Shaanxi province to defend against the invasions by these nomadic peoples from the grasslands in the north. After the State of Qin unified China, the founding emperor dispatched General Meng Tian to lead hundreds of thousands of troops on a sally to the north, driving the enemy north of the Yellow River and recovering all the territory south of it.[32]

In the Han dynasty, the Huns became powerful once more and became the primary threat against China. It was in the Han historical records that the term *Xiong-nu* first appeared. Also Ban Gu and Si-ma Qian both refer to another foreign enemy of China, the *Hu*. *Hu* seems to be a different ethnic group and were referred to as the *Lin-hu* (the *Hu* people of the forest) and the *Dong-hu* (the Eastern *Hu*). Based on the pronunciation of *Hu* they might be of Hunnic race. The Eastern *Hu* lived north of the Yan

---

[31] Si-ma Qian, *Records of the Grand Historian* (*Shi-ji*, completed between 92 BC and 89 BC) Chronicle 50, "Huns" (*Xiong-nu*) (Beijing: Zhonghua Book Company, 2000), 2209-2210. （司马迁：《史记》）

[32] Ban, *Book of Han*, Chronicle 64 I, "Xiong-nu", 2774.

kingdom,[33] in what is present-day northeastern China and were defeated in war by the Huns. According to some linguistics and considering their location, they might have been ancestors of the *Rou-ran* people, who later became the Jurchen-Manchus, and of course, it is also possible that they were those who later became the Khitans or the Mongols. These ethnic groups were all part of the race that originated from the Far East and later dominated the Mongolian steppes, but the facial features of the Huns are the most racially distinctive, just as some pure-blooded Uyghurs today have distinctly Hunnic physical characteristics. It is worth noting that Eastern Hu also possibly included the white race Sibe people. For instance, the Sibe people who founded Northern Wei, according to the *Book of Wei*, [34] indeed originated from the Ga-xian Cave in the Greater Khingan Mountains, and they might have been Lin-hu (Forest Hu) people.

Yuan-he first appears in Chinese historical texts as the transliterated name for the forefather of one of the Uyghur tribes. According to the *New Book of Tang* (*NBoT*), "Uyghurs, their ancestors were Huns, ... and they were called *Gao-che* at the time of *Yuan Wei*. Or called *Chi-le*, and incorrectly called *Tie-le*." Then it concludes that "Yuan-he is also called *Wu-hu*, *Wu-he*, and *Wei-he* in

---

[33] Ban, *Book of Han*, Chronicle 64 I, "Xiong-nu", 2773.
[34] Wei:, *Book of Wei*, Chonicle 88, "Wu Luo Hou 乌洛侯", 1504. "世祖真君四年来朝，称其西北有国家先帝旧墟，石室南北九十步，东西四十步，高七十尺，室有神灵，民多祈请。世祖遣中书侍郎李敞告祭焉，刊祝文于室之壁而还。"

Sui [dynasty]."[35] Note here that the *NBoT* mistakenly refers to Uyghurs as *Gao-che*. The "Yuan-he" was first used in the time of Wei dynasties,[36] which is a history of the Northern Wei (or Later Wei) and Eastern Wei kingdoms, in an account of a battle launched by the Northern Wei in 390: "In the spring, on the *Jia-shen* day of the third month of the fifth year, the founding emperor marched west to conquer. Arriving at the *Lu-hun* Sea, he totally defeated the *Gao-che* tribe of the *Yuan-he*."[37] (*Lu-hun* Sea is Ulungur Lake in Xinjiang's Altai Mountains.) This shows that at that time the Uyghur people were on the western Steppes. According to the inscriptions on the Moyan Chor, Terkin (Tariat or Second Moyan Chor), and Tez or Bogu Khan steles that the Uyghurs erected on the grasslands in the 8th century, the history of the Uyghurs as a nation was divided into three periods, the earliest of which can be traced back to the 4th century the era of the

---

[35] Ou-yang Xiu and Song Qi, *New Book of Tang* (*Xin-tang-shu,* 1060), Chronicle (*Lie-zhuan*) 142 I, "Uyghurs I" (*Hui-gu* I) (Beijing, Zhonghua Book Company, 2000), 4649. （欧阳修、宋祁、范镇、吕夏卿等：《新唐书》）"袁纥者，亦曰乌护，曰乌纥，至隋曰韦纥。"

[36] Ou-yang Xiu and Song Qi, *New Book of Tang*, 142 I.

[37] Wei, *Book of Wei*, "Chronicles of Emperors", No. 2, "The Founding Emperor" (*Di-ji-di-er, Tai-zu-ji*), 15. "五年春三月甲申，帝西征。次鹿浑海，袭高车袁纥部，大破之，……"

Uyghur dyspora at *Gao-che*.[38] This is consistent with Chinese historical records.

Because of this blow from the Northern Wei, the *Yuan-he* Uyghurs in this region were forced to migrate west. According to the research of the French Orientalist James Hamilton, historical records of the Byzantine Empire say that in the period 461-465, envoys from the Sarahur, Uyghur and *On* Oghur were sent for the first time to the Byzantine Empire. These ethnic groups had recently migrated from the east, having been driven out of their homelands by the Sabir people, and later banished by the Avar or Abar people.[39] Uyghur study historian Qian Boquan explains[40] that these Sarahur were the Sari Uyghurs of later times, that is the Yellow Head Uyghurs (Sari means yellow). He also mentions that the Sabir refers to the Sabir (*Xian-bei*) Khanate founded in the waning days of the Eastern Han dynasty in the northeast of present-day China, the Mongolian grasslands, and the Dzungaria Basin. The name "Siberia" for south Russia comes from Sabir. Also, Avars were the *Rou-ran* people,

---

[38] Geng Shimin, *Studies of the Old Turkic Inscriptions* (Beijing: Minzu University of China, 2005), 220. （耿世民：《古代突厥文碑铭研究》）

[39] Qian Boquan, "The Ethnic Origins of the Uyghurs and the Westward Migration of Their Ancestors", *The Western Regions*, No. 3 issue of 1996 (Urumqi: Xinjiang Social Academy), 52-61, citing 52-53. （钱伯泉：《维吾尔族的族源及其先民的西迁》）

[40] Qian Boquan, "The Ethnic Origins of the Uyghurs", 53.

that is those whom Chinese history books derogatorily called "*Ru-ru*", who at this time founded the *Rou-ran* Empire.

Later, the Northen Wei kingdom mentioned in Chinese history, founded the Sibe people, who attacked in 389 and in 390 "the Tribes of Gao-che" and the "Yuan-he tribe" (Uyghur tribe). In the fourth year of Deng-guo (389) in "January the Spring" they attacked all of the Gao-che tribes, and on the Day of Gui-si in February, they arrived at the river of Nv-shui and attacked the *Chi-tu-lin* tribe which was a *Rou-ran* tribe according to Qian Boquan. [41]

At the end of the 4th century and the beginning of the 5th century, Rou-ran people established their Khanate on the Mongolia Grasslands and their territory extended from the Irtysh River at the West and North-eastern part of Tarim Basin, to the Korean border in the East. The first non-white people's nomadic khanate, the *Rou-ran* empire, which had dominated the East Asian (Mongolian) steppes for about 150 years, was defeated in 552 by the Turks, and the Turks occupied the eastern and western steppes, establishing history's first Turkic kingdom. It was the *Rou-ran* people who first used the title "khan" and "khagan". [42] The Turks, Uyghur, Khitan, Jurchen (*Jin*), Mongol, and Manchu (later *Jin*) empires that came later

---

[41] Qian Boquan, "The Ethnic Origins of the Uyghurs", 59. "二月癸巳，至女水，讨叱突邻部，大破之。"

[42] Grousset, *Empire*, 61.

were all updated copies of the *Rou-ran* khanate and their histories played out on *Rou-ran* territory. I agree that the *Rou-ran* people are related to the *Xian-bei* (Hsien-pi) from a linguistic perspective, [43] and that the *Rou-ran* later became the Jurchen, Jin, and Manchu of later years. More specifically, unlike the white people Sabir (*Xian-bei*) (This will be discussed further in a later chapter.), a branch of the *Dong-hu*, who had previously founded the Sabir Empire,[44] the *Rou-ran* were members of the yellow race of East Asia and later became the authentic Jurchen-Manchu, which includes a group called the Sibe (*Xi-bai*) among them even today. I intend to hold that the Sibe (*Xi-bai*) are a group of the descendants of the ancient white Sabir (*Xian-bei*) who were later significantly Jurchen-Manchucized. It seems that all the ethnic groups throughout history that dominated the East Asia steppes in turn can be categorized into these four general ethnicities based on their obvious and different physical and facial features: 1) the *Xiong-nu* and Uyghurs, 2) the Red-White *Di* and Turks, 3) the Jurchen *Jin* and Manchus, and 4) the Khitans and Mongols.

The first mention of "Uyghur" as "Wei-he" in Chinese history is in the *Book of Sui,* written in the early Tang dynasty, which says that they are a branch of the *Tie-le*: "Before they were called *Tie-le*, they were the

---

[43] Grousset, *Empire*, 61.

[44] Qian, "Origins of the Uyghurs", citing 53.

descendants of the *Xiong-nu*, whose ethnicities were the most numerous. From east of the Western Sea, they had spread endlessly along the mountain valleys. Only north of the Yellow River are there *Pu-gu, Tong-luo, Wei-he* [Uyghur], *Ba-ye-gu, Fu-luo*, who together were called *Si-jin*."[45] (The Western Sea is Xinjiang's Bosten Lake, *Tong-luo* is Tonkra, and *Ba-ye-gu* is Bakirku.) Note that it says here that these ethnic groups are known collectively as the *Si-jin* or Irkin, later known as the *Yi-li-jin*. The *Yi-li-jin* or Irkin was a confederation of tribes that were subordinate to a supreme ruler, whose title was also Irkin. *Si-jin* or Irkin is an important clue in understanding the earliest spread of Christianity among the ethnic groups on the grasslands north of the Great Wall, and it will come up again in Chapter Three.

The *OBoT* clearly explains that the Uyghurs were originally the *Tie-le* (*Te-le*), who later became a dominant group on the East Asian Steppes. This historical document describes the Uyghurs as a nomadic people who from the start were excellent and hardy fighters, good at horseback archery, and savage in temperament. They served the khanate of the Turks, frequently engaging in military

---

[45] Wei Zheng, *Book of Sui* (*Sui-shu*; 636), Chronicle 49, "Tie-le" (Beijing: Zhonghua Book Company, 2000), 1260. "铁勒之先，匈奴之苗裔也，种类最多。自西海之东，依据山谷，往往不绝。独洛河北有仆骨、同罗、韦纥、拔也古、覆罗并号俟斤。"（魏徵：《隋书》）

conquests for the Turkic khanate.[46] The meaning of "Turk" (*Tu-jue*) today is powerful, strong, or formidable.[47] The historical name changes for the Uyghurs well-documented in the *OBoT: Uyghurs*: "The *Hui-he* [Uyghurs], they were first the descendants of the *Xiong-nu*. During the Later Wei, they were called the *Tie-le* tribe. Even though they did not appear imposing, their customs were brave and strong, and they leaned and relied on the *Gao-che*. Subjects of the *Tu-jue* [Turks], they have recently been called the *Te-le*."[48] *Gao-che* means "high wheel cart" and refers to the carts with tall wheels that this ethnic group was famous for making and driving. Later Chinese classics, such as the *Old History of the Five Dynasties* also says: "The *Hui-gu* [Uyghurs], their ancestors were of *Xiong-nu* [Huns] race. They were called *Tie-le* as well as *Hui-he* during the Later Wei dynasty."[49]

After the Turks were defeated by Sui dynasty China,

---

[46] Liu, *OBoT*, "Uyghurs", 3535.

[47] Li Sheng, *History and Current Situation of Xinjiang, China* (Urumqi: Xinjiang People Publication House, 2003), 33. （厉声主编：《中国新疆历史与现状》）

[48] Liu, *OBoT*, "Uyghurs", 3535. "回纥，其先匈奴之裔也。在后魏时，号铁勒部落。其象微小，其俗骁强，依托高车，臣属突厥，近谓之特勒。"

[49] Xue Ju-zheng, *Old History of the Five Dynasties* (*Jiu-wu-dai-shi*; 973-974), Foreign Chronicle II, "Uyghurs", (Beijing: Zhonghua Book Company, 2000), 1276. "回鹘，其先匈奴之种也。后魏时，号为铁勒，亦名回纥。"（薛居正：《旧五代史》）

the *Te-le* groups dispersed.⁵⁰ Later, in 605 during the Sui dynasty, for reasons that are unclear, the Turkic Khanate, defeated and plundered the *Te-le* people to which they were subordinate, killing a few hundred of their tribal leaders. This is recorded in the *OBoT*: *Uyghurs*: "In the first year of *Da-ye* [AD 605], *Chu-luo* Khan of the Turkic Khanate attacked the *Te-le* tribes, assessing and plundering much property. Also suspicious of the *Xue-yan-tuo* and other tribes, fearing they would rebel, they rounded up several hundred of their leaders and marshals and slaughtered them all. Therefore, the *Te-le* rebelled. The *Te-le* started out as the *Pu-gu*, *Tong-luo*, *Hui-he*, *Ba-ye-gu*, *Fu-luo-bu*, known collectively as *Si-jin*, and later called *Hui-he* [Uyghur]."⁵¹ Whereupon, the five *Te-le* groups settled "north of the border of *Xue-yan-tuo*, living beside the *Suo-ling* waters".⁵² The *Xue-yan-tuo* (or Syr-Tardouch⁵³), "another different tribe of the *Tie-le*" and as "*Di* people",⁵⁴ is "the most powerful and aggressive tribe

---

⁵⁰ Liu, *OBoT*, "Uyghurs", 3535.

⁵¹ Liu, *OBoT*, "Uyghurs", 3535. "大业元年，突厥处罗可汗击特勒诸部，又猜忌薛延陀，恐为变，遂集其渠帅数百人尽诛之，特勒由是叛。特勒始有仆骨、同罗、回纥、拔野古、覆罗步，号俟斤，后称回纥焉。"

⁵² Liu, *OBoT*, "Uyghurs", 3535. "在薛延陀北境，居娑陵水侧,......"

⁵³ Ma Changshou, *Turks and Turkic Khanate* (Guilin, China: Guangxi Normal University Publishing House, 2006), 48. （马长寿：《突厥人与突厥汗国》）

⁵⁴ Du You, *Comprehensive Institutions* (*Tong-dian*, 801), Bian-fang

33

among all the *Tie-le* tribes, and their cultural customs are basically the same as those of the Turks" [55] so they were possibly a type of *Gao-che* (*Chi-le, Ding-ling*) people who were leaned and relied on by Uyghurs, and were situated on the Tuul River valley. The *Suo-ling* waters refers to the Selenga River. Having apparently congregated here, the Uyghurs continued to follow their nomadic lifestyle and prospered. It was precisely in this area that the Uyghurs founded their new powerful Uyghurish khanate more than a century later.

According to the *NBoT*,[56] the Uyghur khan petitioned the Tang China court in 788 (the fourth year of *Zhen-yuan* of Tang China), asking that the Chinese name of his ethnic group *Hui-he* be changed to *Hui-gu,* a better sounding transliteration; the change was approved. But according to the *OBoT*[57] and the *Old History of the Five Dynasties*,[58] the Uyghur khan Alp Qutlugh Bilga sent an envoy in 809 (the fourth year of the *Yuan-he* reign) to the Tang court to petition the Chinese name change. While the three histories agree that this event took place, the records differ

---

15, " Xue-yan-tuo" (Beijing: Zhonghua Book Company, 1992), 5465-5466. "薛延陀, 铁勒之别部也。"（杜佑:《通典》）

[55] Ou-yang, *NBoT*, "Uyghurs II", 4664. "薛延陀者, ……在铁勒诸部最雄张, 风俗大抵与突厥同。"

[56] Ou-yang, *NBoT*, "Uyghurs I", 4657.

[57] Liu, *OBoT*, "Uyghurs", 3545.

[58] Xue, *Old History of the Five Dynasties*, "Uyghurs", 1276.

as to the year that this occurred. Chinese scholars, however, generally hold that it occurred in 788 (the fourth year of the *Zhen-Yuan* reign),[59] and I agree. It is worth noting that my research found the *OBoT* to be generally more accurate than the *NBoT*.

In summary, it can be concluded that the forefathers of the Uyghurs were the people that China's Qin and Han dynasties called Huns, that the Northern Wei dynasty called the *Yuan-he, Wu-hu,* or *Wu-he* of the *Tie-le* tribes, that the Sui dynasty called the *Wei-he* or *Hui-he* of the *Te-le* tribe, and that the Tang dynasty called the *Wei-he*, the *Hui-he* and *Hui-gu*, all three of which are transliterations of "Uyghur".

The last thing that must be stated is this, the Uyghur people as an ethnic group during the Chinese Sui-Tang dynasties mainly included the "Internal Nine Surnames" clan, led by the Yaghlaqar' clan, and, with the inclusion of the "External Nine Tribes", the Uyghur Khanate was established on this foundation. As the expert on Uyghur history Qian Boquan has incisively summarized: in the mid-8th century, "leader Kutlug I Bilge united the Internal Nine Surnames, combined the External Nine Tribes, conquered the Two Guest Tribes (the Karluks and the Basmyls), and founded the Uyghur Khanate. In this way, the ancient Uyghur ethnic group gradually came into

---

[59] Li Sheng, *Historical and Current Xinjiang, China* (Urumqi: Xinjiang People Publication House, 2003), 40.

being" and from this, the official Uyghur identity formally took shape.⁶⁰

2. Examining and rectifying extant historical narratives: Clarifying the different ethnic attributes of the "Uyghur" and the "Turk", differentiating Uyghurization and Turkification

Attention needs to be paid to the common belief in the traditional scholarly and popular narrative that the Uyghurs are a Turkic people. This narrative was first put forth by Russian scholars (though not all of them), who were the pioneers of the study of the medieval history and civilization of the Uyghurs.⁶¹ However, careful study of Chinese Sui-Tang dynasties historical materials, ancient Turkic and Uyghur stele inscriptions, and Persian historical materials leads to the basic conclusion that this is a misunderstanding and even a misleading notion. In the ancient Chinese historical records, the origin of the Uyghur ethnic identity is clear, whereas the origin of the Turkic ethnic identity is the one that is uncertain. The Chinese historical records of the Sui-Tang dynasties, as

---

[60] Qian, *'Origins of the Uyghurs'*, citing 61.

[61] Albert Kamalov, "The Uyghurs as a Part of Central Asian Commonality: Soviet Historiography on the Uyghurs" in Ildikó Bellér-Hann, M. Cristina Cesàro, Rachel Harris, and Joanne Smith Finley (eds.), *Situating the Uyghurs Between China and Central Asia* (London and New York: Ashgate Publishing, 2007), 31-45, citing 34.

the earliest records that are rich in detail regarding the Turks, clearly present the Uyghurs and the Turks as two different and distinct ethnic groups.

First, the Turks were Hunnified mixed-blood Hu, whose core clan may have been of *Gao-che* and *Rou-ran* blood:

According to the Chinese history *Book of Sui: Turk* (636), it says: "The ancestors of the Turks were the mixed-blood *Hu* people from the *Ping-liang* [present-day Gan-su region] region with their surname being Ashina. After [emperor] Tai-wu of Later Wei destroyed the *Ju-q*u family [kingdom], Ashina led five hundred fleeing families to *Ru-ru*. [Ever since] they have lived at the Golden Mountain for generations and are good at iron work. The Golden Mountain is shaped like a *dou-mou* [military helmet]; the custom was to call the helmet 'turk', so it became their title."[62]

Note that according to the *Book of Wei*,[63] in 439 (the seventh year of the *Cheng-he* or the *Yong-h*e reign of the *Bei-liang* kingdom and the fifth year of the *Tai-yan* reign of the Northern Wei or Later Wei dynasty or kingdom),

---

[62] Wei, *Book of Sui*, "Turks", 1249."突厥之先，平凉杂胡也，姓阿史那氏。后魏太武灭沮渠氏，阿史那以五百家奔茹茹，世居金山，工于铁作。金山状如兜鍪，俗呼兜鍪为'突厥'，因以为号。"

[63] Wei, *Book of Wei*, Chronicle 87, "Lu-shui Hu Ju-qu Meng-xun"（卢水胡沮渠蒙逊）, 1489, 1491-1493.

the emperor Tai-wu of Northern Wei or Later Wei took over the *Bei-liang* kingdom (Northern *Liang*; *Ping-liang*) and forced its king *Ju-qu Mu-jian* to surrender. The *Ju-qu* family was part of the *Lu-shui Hu* people. Right before the defeat, the *Ju-qu* king asked for help from the *Rou-ran* khanate with no avail.

The *Book of Sui* continues: "Or, another version says their ancestors' kingdom was north of the Western Sea, and the kingdom was destroyed by a neighboring kingdom…The Mountains were northwest of Kocho with a cave at the foot…arriving at a flat land with abundant grass stretching for more than 200 *li*",[64] or according to the *Book of Zhou*, "a few hundred *li*" and according to the *History of the Northern Dynasties* "surrounded by the mountains".[65] According to the geographic features described here it is likely that the valley of the Tianshan Mountains lies between present day Urumqi and *Da-ban-cheng*.

---

[64]。Wei, *Book of Sui*, "Turks", 1249. "或云，其先国于西海之上，……其山在高昌西北，下有洞穴，……遇得平壤茂草，地方二百余里。"

[65] Ling-hu De-fen, *Book of Zhou* (*Zhou-shu*, 636), Chronicle 42, "Foreign regions II: Turks" (Beijing: Zhonghua Book Company, 2000), 615. （令狐德棻:《周书》）"周回数百里"; Li Yan-shou, *History of the Northern Dynasties* (*Bei-shi*, 659), Chronicle 87, "Turks; Tie-le" (Beijing: Zhonghua Book Company, 2000), 2181. （李延寿:《北史》）"四面俱山。"

Those are the two theories of the origin of the Turks. Another theory is provided in the Chinese history *Book of Zhou: Turks* (636) and it states: "Another version is that the ancestors of the Turks came from the Kingdom of *Suo*, north of the Huns"[66] The people of Turkey seem to favor this most ambiguous latter explanation. "North of the Huns" here clearly rules out the possibility that the Turks were part of the Huns. The *Book of Zhou: About Yuwen Ce* also says that prior to 542 (the eighth year of the Western Wei dynasty's the *Da-tong* reign), the Turks advanced every year from the west and crossed the frozen Yellow River to invade the northern border area of the Western Wei.[67] The *History of the Northern Dynasties: Turks* (659) includes all three explanations and adds some details to the first: "The ancestors of the Turks lived to the right of the Western Sea and were their own tribe, probably another racial type of Hun, surnamed Ashina."[68]

The three Chinese classics share these points in common: **1.** All mention the Turks as originating from the Ashina clan. **2.** They also all say that the Turks are the

---

[66] Ling-hu, *Book of Zhou*, "Turks", 615. "或云突厥之先出于索国，在匈奴之北。"

[67] Ling-hu, *Book of Zhou*, Chronicle 19, "About Yuwen Ce", 307; Ma, *Turkic Khanate*, 1.

[68] Li, *History of the Northern Dynasties*，"Turks; Tie-le", 2181. "突厥者，其先居西海之右，独为部落，盖匈奴之别种也。姓阿史那氏。"

descendants of a she-wolf impregnated by a human. Although this is clearly not credible, it is the source of the Turkic tradition of the wolf totem. **3.** Since they originated from the Tianshan mountain range northwest of Kocho, the Western Sea referred to in the *Book of Sui* and the *History of the Northern Dynasties* can only be the Bosten Lake in the Korla region of Xinjiang. **4.** After the fall of their kingdom (or tribe), the Turks were the vassals of the *Rou-ran* Khanate of the *Ru-ru* people, lived in the Golden Mountain area, and worked as blacksmiths for the Khanate. The *Ru-ru* of the *Rou-ran* Khanate called them "slave blacksmiths". **5.** They got the name "Turk" because the Golden Mountain is shaped like a military helmet from that period; the custom was to call the helmet "türk" in a local language,[69] so "türk" became their title ("türk" is pronounced "toork").

"Golden Mountain" refers to the Altai Mountains. From a bird's eye view, the shape of the entire mountain range does look like the helmets that were worn in the Northern Wei and late Sui dynasties by Han Chinese and by Turkic soldiers and those of other ethnic groups of the same period, the kind of helmet that covers and protects both ears.[70] In other words, the original meaning of the

---

[69] It is impossible to know whose language is referred to here for "turk" because in the Chinese text it remains vague.

[70] The helmets worn by 7th century Turkic funerary statues of warriors that have been excavated in Kazakhstan are no different in appearance from those worn by funerary statues of Chinese warriors of the Sui-

name "Turk" was derived from the nickname for this kind of helmet, and not what people commonly believe today which is that it might have later evolved to the meaning for "strong and powerful" after the Turks established their khanate.[71]

One French scholar believes that "Turk" comes from "Turukut" in the ancient *Rou-ran* language. This makes obvious sense, even if the common belief today is that it came from the Scythian "Turkut".[72] My view is that it was likely the *Rou-ran* who first gave this somewhat mocking nickname to their "slave blacksmith" the Turks, just as the Han Chinese gave the rather derogatory nickname "Ru-ru" to the *Rou-ran* people. There is a theory that the surname Ashina also originated in the *Rou-ra*n language. This also makes sense, because in modern Manchu-Sibo language the adjective *aishinia* [73] for "gold/golden" can be transliterated as "ah-shi-na" into Chinese, which uses the same characters as those for Ashina. The name "Ashina" is presumably also derived from the Golden Mountain and means Golden Family. The noun *aishin* for "gold" can be transliterated into Chinese as "ai-xin". The "jin" (gold) character in the name of the later Jurchen Jin dynasty and

---

Tang dynasties. Both are this ancient type of helmet that resembled a kind of cooking pot that was used at that time.

[71] Geng, *Inscription*, 1.

[72] Geng, *Inscription*, 1.

[73] In the Sibe (*Xi-bai*) language as it is spoken today in Xinjiang, the pronunciation is closer to *ai-ri-nia*.

in the Aisin Gioro name of the imperial clan of the Jurchen Manchus (in the present-day Sibe language, the imperial name was *"jin-zhao-li"* in Chinese, which means Golden Colander) both came from the word *aishin*.

In view of the widely known academic rigor of the history *Book of Sui*, which was 35 years in the writing, and the fact that the *OBoT* begins its "Chronicle of the Turks" by citing the *Book of Sui* as its primary source, I therefore am inclined to the narrative that the ancestors of the Turks were "mixed-blood *Hu* from the *Ping-liang* region" originally belonging to the Northern Liang kingdom, that is, mixed-blood or biracial *Hu* from the ancient Gansu region. In this way, the Ashina tribe was Hunnifed mixed-blood *Hu*, which is "another racial type of Hun" originally from the *Ping-liang* region, after they migrated to the Golden Mountains and submitted to the Rouran Khanate. After their kingdom was destroyed, some of the mixed-blood *Hu* led by Ashina went and submitted to *Ru-ru* (*Rou-ran*) and settled in the Altai Mountains, likely becoming *Rou-ran*-ized and growing stronger. This would also explain why they became a part of and served the *Rou-ran* kingdom and yet were looked down upon, likely because of the common negative view of "bastards" and/or war refugees in ancient times. Nevertheless, the other two theories about the origins of the Turks should not be ignored.

Regarding the **theory** of the mixed-blood *Hu* being

from the *Ping-liang* region, one needs to note that when Chinese historical materials of this period mention "*Hu* people", they were referring to the white Indo-European ethnic groups, which will be discussed in detail in the second section of this chapter. The *Comprehensive Mirror in Aid of Governance* says, the leader of the An Lu-shan rebellion is "a mixed-blood *Hu* from *Ying* Prefecture",[74] and the *OBoT* says An Lushan was a "mixed-blood *Hu*"; An Lushan himself said, "My father is *Hu*, my mother is Turk."[75] Please note that the *New Book of Tang* pointed out that "An Lu-shan was a Hu person from the Liu city of Ying prefecture" without mentioning his mixed blood from the Turks, and only specifying his physical features as "great and white" meaning big, tall and white.[76] This shows that "mixed-blood *Hu*" refers to those who are part *Hu* and part non-*Hu*, the latter of course includes the Huns, *Rou-ran*, Han Chinese, etc. The *Book of Sui* also mentions that the Turkic khan had sought marriage with the imperial family of its suzerain state, the *Ru-ru* (*Rou-ran*) who rejected the proposal harshly,[77] and the *Book of*

---

[74] Si-ma Guang, *Comprehensive Mirror in Aid of Governance* (*Zi-zhi-tong-jian,* 1084), volume 214: "Tang Ji 30" (Beijing: Zhonghua Book Company, 1976), 6816. "安禄山者，本营州杂胡。"（司马光：《资治通鉴》）

[75] Liu, *OBoT*, Chronicle 54, "Ge-shu-han", 2178. "我父是胡，母是突厥；公父是突厥，母是胡。"

[76] 欧阳修、宋祁：《新唐书》，列传第 150 上，"逆臣上"，第 4853 页。"营州柳城胡也"；"伟而晳"。

[77] Wei, *Book of Sui*, "Turks", 1249.

Sui: *About Pei-ju* says there were "many large groups of *Hu*" among the Turks. [78]

According to Guo Moruo's *Chinese History*, in the waning years of the Eastern Han dynasty, large numbers of Huns migrated south and settled in Gansu, Shaanxi, Inner Mongolia, Shanxi and other areas: "In the time of the Jin dynasty's Emperor Wu, four large migrations into China took place, with several hundreds of thousands [of Hun] being settled in Bing, Yong and other prefectures. At that time, there were also *Hu* people of an ethnic group that was different [from the Hun] who were called mixed-blood *Hu*, the most famous branch of which were the *Lu-shui Hu*."[79] As mentioned earlier the king's family of Northern *Liang* was *Lu-shui Hu*, therefore "Ping-liang mix-blooded Hu" was also related to the *Lu-shui Hu*. The Jin dynasty's emperor Wu Di reigned from 265 to 290. Guo here also says that those "mixed-blood Hu" were a different ethnic group from the Huns. There is another passage in the *Book of Sui* that should not be overlooked: "In the chaos of the final years of the Sui dynasty, countless numbers of Chinese fled [to the Turks, so the Turks] gradually grew in power, becoming a harassing

---

[78] Ma, *Turkic Khanate*, 38; Wei, *Book of Sui*, Chronicle 32, "About Pei-ju", 1063. "其内多有群胡"。

[79] Guo Moruo, *Chinese History*, vol. 3 (Beijing: Peoples Publishing House, 1979), 64. （郭沫若：《中国史稿》）

force in Central Xia."[80] That is to say, the Turkic Khanate became very large and powerful at this time because of the large influx of Han Chinese. In this process, the introduction of large amounts of Han Chinese blood into the Turks was clearly inevitable. According to this record, it entails in this historical period that the non-Hu blood of the Turks was maily from the Han Chinese.

Regarding the other two theories about the origins of the Turks, what needs to be mentioned is that the *Gao-che* are another ethnic group from the Mongolian grasslands who have a legend that they originated from the mating of a woman and a wolf. This is recorded in the *Book of Wei*. Regarding the ethnic tribute of the Gao-che pople, it needs to be explored in detail here.

On the one hand, the common academic view is that the *Gao-che* were the forefathers of the Uyghurs, but I see this as a misunderstanding. The *Records of the Grand Historian* says that the Huns (*Xiong-nu*) of Mao Dun *Chan-yu* (king) conquered the five kingdoms in the north, including the *Ding-ling* kingdom around 200 BC. According to Chinese historical materials and archeological discoveries by the Russians beginning in the

---

[80] Wei, *Book of Sui*, 1258. "隋末乱离，中国人归之者无数，遂大强盛，势陵中夏。"

late 1920s,[81] the *Ding-ling* lived in the area of Lake Baikal and the Yenisei River. After they were conquered, they lived to the left of the Huns, subject to the jurisdiction of the Hun chancellor. The *Wu-sun*, who had also been conquered by the Huns, were living to the right of the Huns. This was the "right arm" of the Huns, under the jurisdiction of the vice chancellor, which China's Han dynasty wanted to break. The *Book of Wei: Gao-che* says, "The *Gao-che* might be remnants of the descendants of the ancient Red *Di*. Originally, they were called *Di-li*, and in the north they are called *Chi-le* while all of *Xia* groups calls them *Gao-che* and *Ding-ling*. Their language is generally the same as the *Xiong-nu (*Huns*)*, with certain minor differences. Their ancestors are said to be the nephew of the *Xiong-nu*."[82]

This points out that the *Gao-che* people were not really Uyghurs, even though their language was basically the same as that of the Huns as a result of their Hunnification. Rather, they are the descendants of the *Chi-di* (red-*di*), that is, they are of the Scythian Indo-European ethnic group and are also called the *Di-li* or *Ding-ling* and the *Chi-le* (or *Ki-le*). It says here that their forefather was

---

[81] Sergei Vladimirovich Kiselev, *The Ancient History of Southern Siberia* (Chinese version volume II; Institute of Ethnic Studies, Xinjiang Academy of Social Sciences, 1985), 48-49, 118.

[82] Wei, *Book of Wei*, "Gao-che", 1561. "高车，盖古赤狄之余种也，初号为狄历，北方以为敕勒，诸夏以为高车、丁零。其语略与匈奴同而时有小异，或云其先匈奴之甥也。"

the nephew of the Huns, which means that after acknowledging their allegiance to the Huns, a political marriage took place between their royal family and a Hun princess. This in a way lines up with the legend in the *Book of Wei* about the *Gao-che* being born from the mating of a wolf and a Hun princess. Moreover, the *Book of Wei* says that "these people loved to sing in loud, high-pitched voices, like a wolf's howl",[83] which aptly describes the *Gao-che* people's penchant for bursting into song. For instance, the famous "Chi-le Shepherd's Song" from the mid-sixth century that was quite popular among the Han Chinese was written by the *Gao-che*.

    The main reason for the academia's misunderstanding that the *Gao-che* were the forefathers of the Uyghurs is that one of the clans of the *Gao-che* was called the "hu-gu",[84] which is another transliteration of "Uyghur". As was mentioned previously, according to the *OBoT*, the Uyghurs during the Later Wei (Northern Wei) dynasty "leaned and relied on the *Gao-che*; subjects of the *Tu-jue* [Turks]", thus echoing the account in the *Book of Wei*. Furthermore, as will be mentioned later, there was a branch of Uyghurs (Sari Uyghurs) who were Indo-Europeans. Just this fact alone could explain who the Uyghurs among the *Gao-che* were: they might have been

---

[83] Wei, *Book of Wei*, "Gao-che", 1561. "故其人好引声长歌，又似狼嗥。"

[84] Wei, *Book of Wei*, "Gao-che", 1561. "其种有狄氏、表纥氏、斛律氏、解批氏、护骨氏、异奇斤氏。"

Uyghur Indo-Europeans who are racially the same as the *Gao-che*.

On the other hand, the Turks, who are the mixed-blood *Hu* originally from *Ping-liang* and who also have a legend tracing their origins to a wolf, may have an interesting relation to *Gao-che* and their *Hu* blood might have primarily come from the *Gao-che*. Also, at this time (the mid-sixth century), the *Gao-che* and the Turks both lived around the Altai Mountains, and the geographic conditions were conducive to a further mixing of bloodlines. In addition, the geographic location of the *Ding-ling*, the forefathers of the *Gao-che*, before they were conquered by the Huns tallies with the *History of the Northern Dynasties* which says that the forefathers of the Turks came from the *Suo* Kingdom north of the Huns. Besides, as mentioned earlier, the *New Book of Tang* says that "the Xue-yan-tuo people, ...their custom is largely similar to the Turks." Because the Xue-yan-tuo probably belonged to the Gao-che racial-ethinc group, it seems that the desciprtion in the Book is quite accurate correspondingly.

In addition, according to the research by the Chinese scholar Duan Lian-qin based on the Chinese classics, such as the *Book of Wei* and *History of the Northern Dynasties*, in 487 about a few hundred thousand people of the *Fu-fu-luo* tribe of *Gao-che,* led by A-fu-zhi-luo, escaped from *Rou-ran* Khanate and migrated to the northwest Kocho region and established the *Gao-che* kingdom (or A-fu-zhi-luo Kingdom).[85] Please note that it also confirms a high possibility of mixed-blood between the Gao-che and the ruler of the Rou-ran people. Later the kingdom expanded further southwest to the area around Karasahr and Bosten Lake, east to the *Shan-shan* area, north to the present-day Urumqi area, and also subjugated the Ko-cho kingdom.[86] It seems that 300 years later when Uyghurs migrated west here they copied the kingdom map of *Gao-che*. In 541, the *Rou-ran* khanate attacked and destroyed the *Gao-che* kingdom.[87] This indicates that the Turks who congregated at the Altai Mountains under the rule of *Rou-ran* after 541 consisted of the mixed-blood *Hu* who should be related to the *Gao-che* people from the two geographic locations: *Ping-liang*, Bosten lake-Tianshan Mountains, and both groups can trace their roots back to the *Suo* kingdom. Therefore, all **three theories** of the origins of the Turks, besides their legendary parts, were likely true.

The description in the *Book of Zhou* of the strange facial features of the Turkic Khanate's third khan *Yan-du* says that "his face is very broad and ruddy, and eyes are

---

[85] Duan Lian-qin, *Ding-ling, Gao-che and Tie-le* (Shanghai: Shanghai People Publishing House, 1988), 218-219.（段连勤:《丁零、高车与铁勒》）

[86] Duan Lian-qin, *Ding-ling, Gao-che and Tie-le*, 226-227, 232-233.

[87] Duan Lian-qin, *Ding-ling, Gao-che and Tie-le*, 252.

like glass."[88] These are clearly the distinct characteristics of the Scythian Indo-Europeans. In addition, from this passage in the *OBoT: Turk I*, "Shi-bi and Chu-luo in appearance look like *Hu* rather than the Turks, so it is doubtful that they are of the Ashina clan... ".[89] It's obvious that even though the Ashina, the core Turkic tribe, were biracial *Hu*, their features were still different from the *Hu* people. The *Xiong-nu* (Huns) or *Rou-ran* (Avars) and Chinese characteristics might have been obvious, but the Turkic tribe as a whole were mainly of Scythian-*Hu* blood (mostly likely of *Gao-che*), along with Hun, *Rou-ran* and Chinese blood. The *History of the Northern Dynasties* also mentions that the Turks' "script resembles *Hu* script",[90] although their language was undoubtedly Hun, which was also the language of the *Te-le*-Uyghur people. Modern linguists commonly refer to the Turk's language as the "Turkic language", mainly because the Turkic Khanate was the first to erect steles with inscriptions in this language.

The record about the physical features shows that the Turks first originated from the mix-blooded Hu people, thus having their primary features from the Hu people and

---

[88] Ling-hu, *Book of Zhou*, "Foreign Regions II", 616. "状貌多奇异，面广尺余，其色甚赤，眼若琉璃。"

[89] Liu, *OBoT*, "Turks I", 3512. "始毕、处罗以其貌似胡人，不类突厥，疑非阿史那族类，……"

[90] Li, *History of Northern Dynasties*, 2183. "其书字类胡"。

minor features from East Asians. The Chinese classics defined them as a Hunnicized group, yet it will be mentioned later that their Hu cultural features were strong. Therefore, their identity sense was inclined towards one of the Hu people which corresponds with all three versions of their origins, especially the last two versions which seem to be narratives from the Turks themselves. Here it implies that they were primarily *Hu* people intermixed with non-*Hu* (Huns, Avars, Chinese, etc.), which aligns with their three possible origins according to the Chinese classics, and they strongly exhibited the characteristics of the *Hu* civilization which reflects their sense of identity. That is why, as mentioned earlier, there were "many large groups of *Hu*" among the Turks. Their *Hu* identity was most likely related to the *Gao-che* from the *Gao-che* kingdom and originally the *Suo* kingdom.

Also, the Kul Tegin stele erected by the Turks says this of the first two khans who founded the Turkic Khanate: "After they ascended to the throne, they founded the nation and established the legal system of the Turks…. They ruled the Kok Turk between heaven and earth."[91] "Kok Turk" or "Blue Turk" is also transliterated into Chinese as "ge-tu-jue" which might have been another name that the Turks called themselves; or it was a term for some special kind of Turk. The meaning of "blue" here is unclear. It could mean "blue eyes" just as we will see later

---

[91] Geng, *Inscriptions*, 121.

in this chapter that "yellow Uyghur" means "Yellow Head Uyghur" (or blonde Uyghur). There is also a blonde "Jurchen" which will be mentioned in Chapter Three.

Second, the Uyghurs are the descendants of the Huns and are part of the *Te-le* (*Tie-le*) ethnic group; they have been mistakenly classified as Turks:

In contrast to the ambiguous narratives about and various possibilities as to the origins of the Turks, the origin of the Uyghurs is very clear. The *Book of Sui* and the *History of the Northern Dynasties*, after introducing the Turks, follows in the same chapter with this introduction of the *Tie-le*: "The ancestors of the *Tie-le* are descended from the Huns. The *Tie-le* branch has more variety than any of the others, spreading endlessly east from the Western Sea along the valleys."[92] Then it lists more than 40 *Tie-le* tribes. Clearly, unlike the Turks who came from the single tribe of Ashina, the *Tie-le* were many tribes and their population was large. As was quoted earlier from the *OBoT*: *Uyghur*: "The *Hui-he*, they were first the descendants of the *Xiong-nu*. During the Later Wei, they were called the *Tie-le* tribe...Subjects of the *Tu-jue* [Turks], they have recently been called the *Te-le*." This clearly explains that the *Tie-le*-Uyghurs are descended from the Huns, while the preceding explanation of the

---

[92] Wei, *Book of Sui*, "Tie-le", 1260; Li, *History of Northern Dynasties*, "Tie-le", 2193. "铁勒之先，匈奴之苗裔也，种类最多。自西海之东，依据山谷，往往不绝。"

Turks presented three possibilities, all of which directly or indirectly ruled out the possibility that the Turks were descendants of the Huns. Furthermore, according to the *Book of Zhou*: "At the time that the *Tie-le* were about to attack the *Ru-ru*, Tu-men of his own volition led his people to confront and thoroughly defeat them [the *Tie-le*], completely subduing more than fifty-thousand family groups."[93] The fact that the Turks were subjects of the *Ru-ru*, and the *Ru-ru* and the *Tie-le* were enemies indirectly shows that the sense of ethnic identity of these two ethnic groups (Turks and Uyghurs) was different.

The totem and the ethnic origins of the Uyghurs were also completely different from that of the Turks. According to the *History of Yuan: Burcuq Art Tigin* and the inscription on the stele of The Meritorious Services of the Iduquts of Kocho erected in 1334 by the Kocho Uyghurs that was written in the Uyghur and Chinese languages, the Uyghur people originated in the Tuul and Selenga river valleys and their ancestors were birthed from a tree;[94] this is clearly not credible. However, the appearance of this explanation of the origins of the

---

[93] Ling-hu, *Book of Zhou*, "Turks", 616. "时铁勒将伐茹茹，土门率所部邀击，破之，尽降其众五万余落。"

[94] Song Lian, *History of Yuan* (*Yuan-shi*, 1370), Chronicle 9, "Ba er shu a er te di jin" (Beijing: Zhonghua Book Company, 2000), 1981. （宋濂：《元史》）

Uyghurs and the name "*wei-wu-er*"[95] on an official Kocho Uyghur self-narrative of the first half of the 14th century undoubtedly refreshed their memories of their ethnic identity and produced a proclamatory effect: clarifying that the Uyghur people and the Turks, who had by then already become the dominant people of Western and Central Asia, were two completely different ethnic groups, even if Europe and Western Asia, including Persia, were at that time already collectively referring to both as Turks, and even if the time for the end of the Turkification process of the various ethnic groups of Central Asia-Xinjiang was fast approaching in the chariots of Islamification.

The early 14th century Persian written Mongol history *Compendium of Chronicles* also says that its introduction of the history of the Uyghur people is based on materials written by the Uyghur people themselves about their own history and their own conclusions. It also gives as examples the following tribes and branches that had originally been Uyghur but were mistaken for branches of the Turks: "the Qarluq [Karluk], the Qalach, the Qipchaq", etc.[96] This means that these three groups

---

[95] Geng Shimin, 'A Study of the Stone Tablet in Uyghur Script about the Meritorious Services of Princes of Gaochang', *Acta Archaeologica Sinica* (Beijing: Chinese Social Science Academy, 1980, No. 4 issue), 515-29, citing 516, 518-519.（耿世民：《回鹘文亦都护高昌王世勋碑研究》）

[96] Thackston, *Compendium of Chronicles*, 74-75.

are Uyghurish, not Turkic. The Chinese texts of the Sui and Tang dynasties essentially confirm this by mentioning Kyrgyz and Kazak as clans of the *Te-le* group[97] which means that the two groups are *Te-le*-ish, not Turkic. To be more specific, the two clans were Hunnified people that were part of the *Te-le* group. The description in the *Compendium* of the Uyghur khan believing in the monotheistic God (Allah)[98] while the Uyghurs were still living on the steppes is clearly not credible, but the description does not mention the name Mohammed. This ambiguity is sufficient to leave open the possibility that it was alluding to the Uyghurs Khan's Christian faith (or Manichaeism). This possibility is not just speculation; the last two chapters of this thesis indirectly support this possibility. Furthermore, the *Compendium* also says, "At the time all [Mongols] were infidels, but with the passage of time they and their families too became monotheists."[99] The last two chapters of this thesis will show that the Mongol royal family and many other Mongols all converted from Shamanism to Christianity. It is important to note that accounts in the *Compendium* are for the most part legends. Important details in some accounts are inconsistent and even contradictory, especially with regards to geographic location, which is very disordered. This is a common problem with Muslim historical

---

[97] Qian, "Origins of the Uyghurs", citing 56.

[98] Thackston, *Compendium of Chronicles*, 28-29.

[99] Thackston, *Compendium of Chronicles*, 29.

materials.

The Uyghurs and the Turks are different in other important ways. For instance, there are differences in the geographic location of their distribution. According to the *Book of Sui*, the *Tie-le*, of whom the Uyghurs were a part, as descendent of the Hun not only were comprised of many tribes but also clearly inherited the territory that the Huns had occupied in the previous approximately eight centuries: spanning Eurasia, from north of the Yellow River in the east, south of Lake Baikal to southwest of the Altai Mountains in Xinjiang, west of Hami, as well as the area south of the Tianshan mountain range north and east of Yanqi (Karashahr). To the west, this territory spread to north of the Central Asian Kingdom of Kang (Samarkand), the southern part of the Volga River, east and west of the Caspian Sea, and even approaching the Byzantine region.[100] Also, even though the customs of the *Tie-le* (*Te-le*) and the Turks are on the whole similar, they have differences that are worth examining. The *Book of Sui* says that the Turks "had approximately the same customs as the Huns", and "bury the ashes" of their dead after cremation,[101] while *Te-le* "customs are approximately the same as the Huns', except that after marriage, the groom lives with the bride's family until a boy or girl is born and nursed, then the couple returns to his home; also they bury

---

[100] Wei, *Book of Sui*, "Tie-le", 1260.

[101] Wei, *Book of Sui*, "Turks", 1250.

[the bodies of] their dead, which is another difference."[102] This shows the differences between the two groups in marriage and other life rituals, and is clearly valuable information. From the descriptions of Turkic customs in the *Book of Sui*, the dominance of Hun tradition is evident, but it also says, "In the month of May, many sheep and horses are slaughtered, to sacrifice to the Sky [Heaven]. The men like to play chess, the women play kickball. They drink fermented mare's milk, and when drunk they sing songs to each other",[103] as if to show again the customs of the Indo-European *Gao-che* people enjoying this kind of party and gathering.[104]

In general, although the Turks were mixed-blood *Hu*, and despite the fact that their core tribe likely originated from *Gao-che Hu* blood, and mixed blood from the Huns, Rou-ran and Han Chinese, their main language, customs and systems were still in the Hun tradition. This is why the *Book of Zhou* and the *History of the Northern Dynasties*

---

[102] Wei, *Book of Sui*, "Tie-le", 1261."其俗大抵与突厥同，唯丈夫婚毕，便就妻家，待产乳男女，然后归舍；死者埋殡之，此其异也。"

[103] Wei, *Book of Sui*, "Turks", 1250."五月中，多杀羊马以祭天，男子好樗蒲，女子踏鞠，饮马酪取醉，歌呼相对。"

[104] Wei, *Book of Wei*, "Gao-che", 1561, 1563. 高车人"男女大小皆集会，平吉之人则歌舞作乐，……""高宗时，五部高车合聚祭天，众至数万。大会,走马杀牲，游歌吟忻忻，其俗称自前世以来无盛于此。"

point out that they "might be another racial type of Hun". The problem here is that the Hun's cultural tradtion could have been from either the Hunnicized Gao-che or from the Huns and Gao-che mixing their blood and becoming Turks. It is not clear. Besides, some Chinese and Japanese scholars believe *"Te-le"* is an incorrect translation of "Turk", that the two are the same; this is clearly far-fetched but it has already become a mainstream view. The contemporary scholar of ethnic history Duan Lianqin had this to say about this view: "In the historical texts of the Sui-Tang dynasties, the *Tie-le* were the *Tie-le*, the Turks were the Turks, the two were clearly differentiated. No *Tie-le* tribe was ever called Turk, and no Turk tribe was ever called *Tie-le*."[105] Noted contemporary historian Cen Zhongmian also holds this view, and also says that the pronunciation of these two terms is clearly different.[106]

According to the *OBoT* and *NBoT*,[107] the eldest son of the Uyghur khan Moyan Chor, Ye-hu in 757 (second year of the Tang dynasty's *Zhi-de* reign) came to the aid of Tang China, launching a joint military operation with the famous Chinese general Guo Ziyi to put down the An Lu-shan rebellion. In 759 (the second year of the Tang

---

[105] Duan Lianqin, *Xue-yan-tuo in the Sui and Tang Dynasties* (Xi'an: Sanqin Publishing House, 1988), 7. 段连勤:《隋唐时期的薛延陀》

[106] Duan Lianqin, *Xue-yan-tuo in the Sui and Tang Dynasties*, 7.

[107] Liu, *OBoT*, "Uyghurs", 3537, 3539; Ou-yang, *NBoT*, "Uyghurs I", 4652-4653.

dynasty's *Gan-yuan* reign), the Uyghur prince "gu-chuai-te-le" led troops to the aid of the Tang dynasty, again in a joint military operation with General Guo. The seventh line of the inscription on the eastern face of the Uyghur Moyan Chor stele says, in the first-person voice of his father Moyan Chor, "I gave my two sons the titles Yabghu and Shad."[108] And the inscription on the north face of the Uyghur Terkin stele says in the third line, "I, the Tangri Khan, and my sons Bilgä Tarqan and Qutlugh Bilgä Yabghu".[109] (Note that he uses the princes' titles here rather than their names.)

Putting together the information in the historical materials in the two languages, it's clear that the same prince is being referred to, that is, the eldest son of Moyan Chor, who led troops twice to the aid of the Tang dynasty, and on both occasions was accompanied by Chancellor and General Di-de. The "-tlugh" in the prince's name in *OBoT* and *NBoT* is transliterated *"Te-le"*, the same transliteration as the name of the ethnic group *Te-le*. This is not likely a coincidence. I therefore propose that the English transliteration of the *"Te-le"* people's name be "Tlugh" and the people are "Tlughur" which includes

---

[108] Geng, *Turkic Inscriptions*, 198; Shang Yanbing, "An Initial Probing into the Political System of Ancient Uighur Khanate in Northern Mongolia", *NW Journal of Ethnology*, No. 1 Issue of 1995 (Lanzhou, China: Northwest University for Nationalities, 1995), 13-25, citing 20. （尚衍斌：《漠北回鹘汗国政治体制初探》）

[109] Geng, *Turkic Inscriptions*, 211, 217.

Uyghur people. I also propose different *Te-le*-ish tribes as "Tlughish" tribes which distinguishes them from the Turkic or Turkish group, Khitan group, Mongol group, Jurchen group, *Hu* group and *Di* group. Therefore, Tlughurs are Hunnic, and Uyghur is a Tlughish group, not Turkic.

Because the Turks were the first to have a written language, all the other Hunic- Tlughish speaking ethnic groups,[110] including the Uyghurs who were subjects of the Turkic Khanate —"Their ancestors were descendants of the Huns"[111] — are all collectively referred to as the Turkic language family, just as many European ethnic groups are collectively referred to as the Romance language family. One scholar has pointed out that "Turkic" refers to "the broader ethnic and linguistic category which includes Turkish, Uyghur, Uzbek, Kazakh, Kyrgyz and others".[112]

Third, the Turks and the Uyghurs were centuries-long enemies and at war for more than 200 years:

According to Hamilton, a report by the Byzantine-bound Turkic Khanate envoy Zemarchos said that the Uyghurs who had moved west from the Altai Mountain to the area north of the Caucasus mountain range and west of

---

[110] Geng, *Turkic Inscriptions*, 3.

[111] Liu, *OBoT*, "Uyghurs", 3535. "回纥，其先匈奴之裔也。"

[112] Millward, *Crossroads*, 31.

the Volga River had by 569 already submitted to the Turkic Khanate. On his return journey, this envoy traveled through this area. Also, in 576, the Turkic Khan announced to the Byzantine envoy Valentin that he had already conquered the "un yghur" people.[113] In 598, according to a letter from the West Turkic khan, the Turkic Khanate had already conquered the *Rou-ran* (Avar) people and the MoKri people, then also conquered the "Ogor" people. The "Ogor" ethnic group, a numerous and war-loving people, was one of the largest ethnic groups. They lived further east, in the Irtysh River area.[114] That is to say, these Uyghurs who lived in the east were the "Yuan-he" and the "Hu-gu" who stayed behind in the Altai mountain range during the period of the Northern Wei kingdom, and were the "Wu-he" and "Wu-hu" (Wu-he) in the Northern Wei and Sui-Tang dynastic classics; the former were of the *Gao-che* tribes and the latter were of the *Te-le* tribes.[115] These Uyghurs in the east appear to be different from the westward-migrated Uyghurs in the Caucasus-Volga regions; the former were predominantly yellow or even dark skinned (they were descendants of the Huns), while the latter might have been predominantly white, just like the aforementioned two kinds of Sabir (*Xian-bei*) people.

---

[113] Qian, "Origins of the Uyghurs", citing 53.

[114] Qian, "Origins of the Uyghurs", citing 53.

[115] Qian, "Origins of the Uyghurs", citing 56, 59. "袁纥氏"、"护骨氏"；"韦纥"、"乌护"（乌纥）。

The *Book of Sui: Turk* says: "In the latter years of the Northern Wei [dynasty], the Ilikhan [of the Turks] mustered troops to attack the *Tie-le*, thoroughly defeating them [the Tie-le], and completely subduing more than fifty-thousand family groups...." The Northern Wei dynasty followed the Wei dynasty and was in power from 386 to 534. As mentioned earlier, according to the *Book of Sui: Te-le*, the Turks ruled over, used and even harshly oppressed the *Te-le* people, of which the Uyghurs were a part. The Turks even attacked *Te-le* people and massacred a few hundred of *Te-le* Tribal leaders in 605. The *Te-le* and their subjects the *Xue-yan-tuo* tribe responded with fierce resistance to the Turks. Then, the *Te-le* under the leadership of Mo-he Khan and from their base in the eastern part of the Tianshan mountain range, defeated the Turks and started to grow and become powerful. In 607 (the third year of the Sui dynasty's *Da-ye* reign), they sent their first envoy to Sui dynasty China.[116] After the *Te-le* victory over the Turks, the Turks and the Uyghurs thenceforth were constantly at war. According to the *OBoT: Uyghurs*, in 627 (the first year of the Tang dynasty's *Zhen-guan* reign), the Uyghurs and *Xue-yan-tuo* attacked and soundly defeated the Eastern Turks.[117]

In the inscriptions on the steles that the Turks themselves erected, they repeatedly and consistently referred to the ceaseless wars with each other. The Turks'

---

[116] Wei, *Book of Sui*, "Tie-le", 1261.
[117] Liu, *OBoT*, "Uyghurs", 3535.

inscription on the Tonyuquq stele, erected in 716-725[118] says that the Turks went to war five times with the Oghuz to the north, killing a great number of them before finally conquering them.[119] The narrative in the inscription on the Kul Tegin stele, erected in 732[120] says the Nine Surnames Oghuz were the enemies of the Turks[121] and explained, "The Nine Surnames Oghuz originally were my own people, but due to cosmic chaos, they became our enemies, and we went to war with them five times in one year."[122] The inscription on the famous Bilga Khan stele, erected in 735,[123] also proclaims their achievements, saying the Turks had killed the Baz Khan of the Nine Surnames Oghuz and erected a stone commemorating the killing. Another time, they followed the Selenga River and attacked the Uyghurs, destroying their khanate court and sending the Uyghur khan Eltabr and more than 100 others fleeing to the east.[124] These events occurred roughly between 716 and 734.[125] Later, it will be proved that the Nine Surname Oghuz were the Nine Surname Uyghurs.

---

[118] Geng, *Turkic Inscriptions*, 92.

[119] Geng, *Turkic Inscriptions*, 96, 98, 105.

[120] Geng, *Turkic Inscriptions*, 115.

[121] Geng, *Turkic Inscriptions*, 124.

[122] Geng, *Turkic Inscriptions*, 133.

[123] Geng, *Turkic Inscriptions*, 148.

[124] Geng, *Turkic Inscriptions*, 154, 163.

[125] Geng, *Turkic Inscriptions*, 148.

The same theme was presented in the inscriptions on the steles that the Uyghurs themselves erected. For its part, the Terkhin stele erected in 753-756[126] describes how they attacked the Turks, destroyed the Turkic Khanate, and overthrew Turkic rule.[127] The inscription on the famous Karabalghasun stele, erected in 814, records how the Uyghur people, "a few years after the Basmyl khan Ashina [began his] revolution [against Turks], we re-established our old kingdom."[128] Note here that it says they re-established their kingdom from olden times; they did not found their kingdom for the first time. Also note that the surname of the Basmyls' khan was Ashina, which means he was also a Turk. This then explains why after they re-founded their khanate, the Uyghurs immediately allied with the Uyghurish Karluks to attack the Basmyls, forcing them to flee to the Western Regions.[129] The Turks' Bilga Khan Inscription confirms this, saying, "The Idiqut of the Basmyls is from my clan."[130]

Note that according to the translation by Geng Shimin, an expert in ancient Turkic, the Bilga Khan and

---

[126] Geng, *Turkic Inscriptions*, 207.

[127] Geng, *Turkic Inscriptions*, 213.

[128] Lin Gan and Gao Zihou, *Uyghur History* (*Hui-he Shi*; Hohhot: Inner Mongolia People's Publishing House, 1994), 402-403. （林幹、高自厚：《回纥史》）

[129] Liu, *OBoT*, "Uyghurs", 3537.

[130] Geng, *Turkic Inscriptions*, 159.

the Kul Tegin inscriptions say, respectively, "The Nine Surname Oghuz originally were my own people"[131] and "The Nine Surname Oghuz are my people",[132] but other versions translate it as "Nine Surname Oghuz originally were my same clan" (Bilga Khan inscription)[133] and "The Nine Surname Oghuz is my same clan" (Kul Tegin inscription),[134] thus resulting in the mistaken belief among Chinese scholars that they were also Turks. It must be recognized that the aforementioned Chinese historical materials from the Sui and Tang dynasties and the Turkic and Uyghur stele inscriptions all say that after the Turks established their khanate, they started to rule the *Te-le-*Uyghur people, for at least a century and a half.[135] That is to say, the *Te-le*-Uyghurs had indeed once been people of the Turkic Khanate, except that they occasionally rebelled. This shows, therefore, that Geng's translation is the most accurate. What's important is that the information in the Sui and Tang dynasty historical materials and the Uyghur inscriptions are consistent with each other. In addition, Russian Orientalist Vladimir Minorsky pointed out that 'It is pretty clear that the term "Nine Oghuz" did not apply to the *Türk* nucleus of the Eastern Türk federation, nor to the

---

[131] Geng, *Turkic Inscriptions*, 160.

[132] Geng, *Turkic Inscriptions*, 133.

[133] Duan, *Xue-yan-tuo*, 9.

[134] Ma, *Turkic Khanate*, 6.

[135] Geng, *Turkic Inscriptions*, 194.

Ten Arrows of the Western Türk federation'.[136]

Summary: The need to clarify the relevant terms that cause identity confusion about the Turks and the Uyghurs

In summary, the *Te-le* (*Tie-le*), of whom the Uyghurs were a part, were the authentic descendants of the Huns; the Turks, on the other hand, were not the descendants of the Huns but were merely Hunnified "mixed-blood Hu". Turks in their early period were a marginalized group who were held in contempt by other ethnic groups in the East Asia Steppes. Their bloodline early on was probably mainly *Gao-che* white *Hu* people, mixed with *Xiong-nu* (Huns), *Rou-ran* (Avars) and Chinese, so at best they can only be called "another racial type of Hun". Therefore, the physical characteristics of the two should be different, and the next chapter will take up this discussion. Later, the Turkified Islam of Central Asia resulted in the further use of the generic term "Turkic" for these Central Asian-Xinjiang ethnic groups, and through the process of Islamification, the Uyghurs, Kazakhs, Kyrgyz and other Tlughish, Uyghurish and Indo-European ethnic groups underwent Turkification. Ultimately the terms "Turk" and

---

[136] Vladimir Minorsky, "Tamim ibn Bahr's Journey to the Uyghurs", *Bulletin of the School of Oriental and African Studies, University of London*, Vol.12, No. 2 (Published by: Cambridge University Press on behalf of School of Oriental and African Studies, 1948), 275-305, citing 286.

"Turki" were designated for Uyghurs after they were Islamified. This thesis uses only "Turkic-speaking" people to refer to Uyghurs and other related groups.

By the early 20th century, the pan-Turkish and pan-Islam propaganda of the modern-day "mixed blood *Hu*", the Turkish people, had further drowned out the true ethnic identity of the Uyghurs and their brethren the Uzbeks, and this continues to this day. The Uyghurs historically have tried to rid themselves of Turkification, and have never given up their attempts and struggles to maintain their own independent ethnic identity and civilization. Of course, historically, the subject of the grand Uyghurization of the Xinjiang region was mainly the Indo-Europeans; the subject of the Turkification of Central Asia were the Indo-Europeans, the Uyghurs, the Kazakhs, the Kyrgyz and the Mongols; and the great sinification of East Asia by the Han Chinese assimilated the Jurchens Manchu, the Khitans, some Mongols and some white Indo-Europeans. These were all instances of dissimilation of different ethnic groups and their civilizations.

What must be explained is this: based on the above arguments, this thesis will take great care in differentiating the use of Uygherization and Turkification, and regard both as the continuation of the process of Hunnification and the development of the two directions that the process branched into. The term Hunnification is more correct than the term Turkification. On the basis of this definition, the Xinjiang region and Uzbekistan are both examples of the success of Uyghurization, while Kazakhstan and Kyrgyzstan are models of successful Turkification. Early Muslim historical records called the mid-9th century Kocho Uyghur Khanate, established after the Uyghurs fled west, "Uyghuristan";[137] this is clearly quite an expert term, even though prior to the Islamification of the Uyghurs their kingdom should be called the Uyghur Khanate. By the mid-17th to early 19th centuries, even the Kashgar region was also called "Uyghuristan".[138]

In the early 19th century, the European-Russian writers began to call Xinjiang "Chinese Turkestan" (or "East Turkestan") in contrast to the Uzbekstan the Central Asia "Russian Turkestan" (or "West Turkestan"), [139] though a few of them denied having "any Turkic element in Uyghur history" [140] which is correct, because they treated Uyghurs as the descendants of Tangut people,[141] which is incorrect (The Tangut people will be referred to in later chapters as the white Indo-Europeans). This catalyzed the invention of the title of "the two short-lived 'Eastern Turkestan Republics' of the 1930s and 1940s" by

---

[137] Millward, *Crossroads*, 52; Brophy, *Uyghur Nation*, 23.

[138] Brophy, *Uyghur Nation*, 27.

[139] Kamalov, "Soviet Historiography on the Uyghurs", citing 33–34; Millward, *Crossroads*, ix.

[140] Brophy, *Uyghur Nation*, 48.

[141] Brophy, *Uyghur Nation*, 48.

the Uyghur *jihad* revolutionists in Kashgar and Ili, Xinjiang.[142]

Therefore, the fact that "East Uyghuristan" or "Chinese Uyghuristan" were not used clearly was due to the challenge posed by and oppression imposed by the process of Turkification to the status of Uyghurization, and was a continuation of the geo-political jockeying between the Turks and the Uyghurs that began in the 6th century. In the process, post-Islamified Uzbekistan should have been called "West Uyghuristan", but it was called "West Turkestan" and "Russian Turkestan", due to the religious and political amnesty offered to the Uzbeks, who should be called western Uyghurs. This will be further discussed later in this paper.

3. The rise and fall of the Uyghurs in East Asia: the Orkhon Khanate Uyghurs (744-848)

Soon after, another kingdom arose on the steppes of East Asia. In 744, the nomadic Uyghurs based in the region of the Selenga and Orkhon rivers attacked and defeated the second Turkic Khanate, which had ruled the Uyghurs for 50 years, according to the Moyan Chor inscription (also referred to as the Shine-usu inscription)

---

[142] Millward, *Crossroads*, ix.

erected about 759, [143] on the Mongolian steppes and supplanted it, establishing the Uyghur Khanate, also known as the Orkhon Uyghur Khanate. The Uyghurs were aided in this by the Uyghrish Karluks (*Ge-luo-lu*) from the area of Lake Balkhash, the Emil River (or Emin River; in Xinjiang's Tarbagatay or *Ta-cheng* basin) and the Ili River basin, and by the Basmyls (*Ba-xi-mi*) who were possibly Turkic from the Beshbalik regions. The official reign name of the Uyghur Khanate was Bilga and its territory extended west to the Altai mountains in North Xinjiang and east to the Khingan Range. The following year, Tang China emperor Xuan-zong conferred on the Uyghur khan *Gu-li Pei-luo* from the Yaghlaqar clan, whose throne title was Qutlugh Bilga Kul Khan, the title of *Huai-ren* Khan, [144] acknowledging the new khanate as China's neighbor to the north. This neighbor would be a source of aid and of trouble in the following century.

The Uyghur Khanate dominated the East Asian steppes for a century, coinciding with the golden age of Chinese history: The Tang dynasty. In terms of civilizational advancement and national power, China far surpassed all others in East Asia. The two most militarily powerful nations, the Uyghur khanate and Tang China, established close but complex diplomatic relations. In the process, the relationship between the Uyghur people and the Tang Chinese was sometimes close, sometimes on bad

---

[143] Geng, *Turkic Inscriptions*, 193-194.
[144] Li, *Xinjiang*, 36; Grousset, *Empire*, 113-114.

terms, mainly guided by political, economic and even religious interests.

During the century of their khanate, the Uyghur people built upon the civilizational foundation that they inherited from Huns and the Turkic Khanate and learned from the civilizations of the Sogdians of Central Asia and China. According to a stele erected in 759 praising the achievements of the second khan, Yaghlaqar Moyan Chor (Moyanchur) Khan, and written in the first person, this khan was keen to build palaces. The inscription on this stele, known as the Shine-usu Inscription or Moyan Chor Inscription, said: "I had people build a palace, people put up palace walls." [145] This khan built palaces in four different locations and in one city which is mentioned specifically on the Inscription: "I had the Sogdian [*Su-te*] and the Tabghach[146] [Chinese] build a luxurious city on the Selenga" River.[147]

The first city on the grasslands was reportedly built by the *Rou-ran* (Avar) people, situated in the Orkhon River valley. The capital city of Mubalik or Kara Balgasun (meaning "big tiger city", also called Ordubaliq, meaning "royal city"), built by the Uyghur khanate in 751, was situated in a river valley on the upper reaches of the

---

[145] Geng, *Turkic Inscriptions,* 198.

[146] Chinese transliteration is *Tao-hua-shi*. （桃花石）

[147] Geng, *Turkic Inscriptions*, 203.

Orkhon River; beginning in 759/761,[148] or 762/763[149] it became the headquarters of Manichaeism in East Asia. Chinese scholars generally agree that it was in 763 (the second year of the *Bao-ing* reign of Tang China) that the Uyghurs brought Manichaeism to their khanate.[150] East Syriac Christianity (Nestorianism) meanwhile had already become popular in Tang China before and during this time (635-845), even for a time gaining the upper hand in the court at Chang'an (today, it is the city of Xi'an, famous for its Terracotta Warriors). The history of the religious attribute of the Uyghur people's identity will be explored in the next chapter.

In the Uyghur Khanate were many *Hu* people who were Sogdians (many of whom were Manichaean) and profoundly influenced the politics of the khanate. Remember that there were "many large groups of *Hu*" (likely *Gao-che Hu*) that used to be in the Turk's Khanate. This was also the principle way in which the Sogdian civilization influenced the Uyghur people. Some Uyghurs

---

[148] Larry Clark, "The Conversion of Bügü Khan to Manichaeism" in International Conference on Manichaeism et al., *Studia Manichaica: IV. Internationaler Kongress zum Manichäismus, Berlin, 14.-18. juli 1997* (Berlin: Akademie Verlag, 2000), 83-123, citing 115.

[149] Clark, "The Conversion of Bügü Khan to Manichaeism", 86.

[150] Li Shuhui, "Discussing the Time of the Perishment of Manichaeism", *Studies in World Religions*, No. 4 issue of 2008 (Beijing: Chinese Academy of Social Sciences), 110-17, citing 111. 李树辉：《试论摩尼教消亡的时间》，刊登于《世界宗教研究》。

went to study in Tang China and took up government posts there, becoming conversant with Tang Chinese civilization. For example, the Karabalghasun Inscription, on a stele erected in 814 and discovered in the ruins of the capital of the Uyghur Khanate in 1889 by a Russian explorer, is written in three languages: Uyghur, Chinese and Sogdian.[151] The Chinese version was written by a Uyghur.

The Uyghur Khanate's powerful military profoundly impacted the geopolitics of East Asia. We know from the fragmentary records of the Shine-usu (Moyan Chor) Inscription, the Tez Inscription (761-762), and the Terkhin Inscription (756-757) and by combing through their translations that sometime around 754-755, Yaghlaqar Moyan Chor Khan (Chinese title: *Ying-wu* khan) led the Uyghur people on a westward expedition in the Junggar basin, defeating their former allies along the northern branch of the Silk Road at the territory of "the Basmyls inhabited the environs of Beshbalik in the eastern Tianshan" region and the Karluks "west of the Basmils and south of the Altay, bordering on the territory of the Yagma people", resulting in the Karluks fleeing west to the Zhetysu region [152] while the whereabouts of the Basmyls is unknown. In 755-756, the khan sent his two sons, one of whom would later be the Tengri Bogu Khan

---

[151] Lin Gan and Gao Zihou, *Uyghur History*, 396, 398, 402-403.

[152] Larry Clark, "The Conversion of Bügü Khan to Manichaeism", 107, 109-110.

(Chinese title: *Ying-yi* khan), to attack the cities of the Tarim Basin at the foot of the south side of the Tianshan mountain range—that is, the area on the southern branch of the Silk Road—attacking the Yagmas, the Tang Chinese, and the Sogdians.[153] As a result, the Uyghurs controlled the use of the Silk Road and tax collection in central-eastern Tianshan-Tarim regions.

Also, in 756, likely after the westward expedition, the Uyghurs initiated another military action on a different frontier. When the An Lushan Rebellion (or the An-shi Rebellion as it is called in Chinese history) erupted in Tang China, the Uyghurs swiftly sent their army and helped the Tang court successfully put down the uprising after some years. In politics and diplomacy, Tang China also inherited from and carried on the effective strategy of China's Han dynasty of using the political marriages of its royal princesses to ally with and win the loyalty of the Uyghurs. This Tang dynasty strategy was employed not just with the Uyghurs but also with the Tibetans. Beginning in the mid-7th century until the 820s, the Uyghur Khanate and the Kingdom of Tibet (*Tu-bo*) were frequently at war, fighting over the part of the Silk Road cities along the Tarim Basin at the foot of the south side of and the eastern part of the Tianshan mountain range, with the Uyghurs sometimes carrying out military attacks against the Tibetans on behalf of the Chinese Tang

---

[153] Clark, "The Conversion of Bügü Khan to Manichaeism", 112-113.

dynasty.

According to the *OBoT*, in 764 (the 2nd year of the *Guang-de* reign), the allied troops of the Uyghurs and Tang China defeated the Tibetans, and in 791 (the 7th year of the *Zhen-yuan* reign), Uyghur troops alone defeated the Tibetan and the Karluks, sending many captives to the Chinese court in Chang'an.[154] In 821 (the 1st year of the *Chang-qing* reign), the new Uyghur khan married a Tang Chinese princess Tai-he, and as an expression of gratitude and loyalty, the khan, on his own initiative, sent his troops to attack the Tibetans as a way to welcome the Tang princess.[155] Over the course of the Tang dynasty, about six princesses were married off to Uyghur khans and three of them were daughters of emperors.

A discrepancy in the Chinese historical records is the date of the fall of the Uyghur Khanate. The common belief among scholars is that the Uyghur khanate fell in 840, but that specific year is actually an understandable error. According to the *OBoT*, "In the first year [of the *Hui-chang* reign], the *Xia-ga-si* defeated the *Hui-gu*, capturing Princess Tai-he."[156] This is a reference to the killing of the

---

[154] Liu, *OBoT*, "Uyghurs", 3542, 3545. "七年八月，回纥遣使献败吐蕃、葛禄于北庭所捷及其俘畜。"

[155] Liu, *OBoT*, "Uyghurs", 3545-3546. "长庆元年……回鹘奏："以一万骑出北庭，一万骑出安西，拓吐蕃以迎太和公主归国。""

[156] Liu, *OBoT*, "Uyghurs", 3547. "初，黠戛斯破回鹘，得太和公

Uyghur khan by the white Indo-European nomadic Khyagas (*Xia-ga-si*, also known as Kyrgyz, or Kirgiz) in the first year of the *Hui-chang* reign (841) of the Tang dynasty, the capture of the Tang dynasty princess Tai-he, who had been married for many years to the Uyghur khan, and the overthrow of the Uyghur empire that had dominated the Mongolian steppes for a century. Tang dynasty emperor *Wu-zong* Li Yan ascended the throne in 840, but that year was still the fifth year of the *Kai-cheng* reign of the previous emperor, *Wen-zong* Li Ang, while the opening year of his *Hui-chang* reign would have been the following year, that is, 841. The *NBoT* also corroborates the fall of the Uyghur empire as happening shortly after the Tang emperor *Wu-zong* ascended the throne (it uses the term *e'er*, which means "very soon"), but it does not specify whether it was that same year or the following year. In the *Old Book of Tang*, "About Wuzong Emperor", it says clearly: "In the first year of *Hui-chang*, ... in August, the Uyghur Khan Uge [Wu-jie] sent an envoy reporting the trauma, saying that their kingdom was attacked by the Khyagas [Xia-ga-si] and that after the former Khan died, the tribes and the people chose him to be the Khan." [157] Besides, in the *Old History of the Five Dynasties*, this historical event is clearly described as happening in the first year of *Hui-chang*: "In the first year

---

主。"

[157] 刘昫：《旧唐书》，本纪第 18 上，"武宗"，第 399-400 页。"会昌元年……八月，回鹘乌介可汗遣使告难，言本国为黠戛斯所攻，故可汗死，今部人推为可汗。"

of *Hui-chang*, its kingdom was invaded by the *Xia-ga-si*, the tribes created disturbances, and moved their encampments to between *Tian-de* and *Zhen-wu*."[158] The Great Anti-Buddhist Persecution took place in the fifth year of the *Hui-chang* reign, that is, in 845 as commonly agreed and not in 844, which means 840 was not the first year of the *Hui-chang* reign. Therefore, the conclusion is that 841 should be the correct year of the Uyghur Khanate's fall.

Here it should be noted that with the social scientific research methodology in history, one always needs to trace back those primary original resources for answers, especially through textual analysis. After WWII, and especially after the 1960s, the scholars in China and the Western world who majored in East Asia and Central Asia studies seemed to lean more towards doing research based on second resources and no longer paid much attention to ancient Chinese primary materials. To quite a serious degree, the contemporary academia has ignored the concrete fine methodology on historical studies started by the founders of Sinology who were European, Russian, Chinese and Japanese scholars and Signologists, and who carefully and thoroughly studied the primary and original historical texts and archaeology discoveries, corrected the existing research results, and presented new discoveries.

---

[158] Xue Juzheng, *Old History of the Five Dynasties*, 1276. "会昌初，其国为黠戛斯所侵，部族扰乱，乃移帐至天德、振武间。"

Regarding the time of the westward Uyghur migration, this also needs careful examination. The *Comprehensive Mirror in Aid of Governance* says, "Since the invasion and decline that began in the fourth year of the *Kai-cheng* reign [839], Uyghurs from many tribes have been moving west."[159] This makes it clear that Uyghurs were already moving west in 839, but the large-scale westward migration did not formally begin until after the fall of the khanate in 841. After their khanate fell, the Uyghurs were forced to migrate south and west. According to the *OBoT*: "The Uyghur Chancellor Sa-zhi brought six men, that is, his nephew Pang-te-qin [Pang the *Tegin*] and his five sons, including Nan-lu and E-fen, and led 15 tribes that fled west to *Ge-luo-lu*, one branch headed for *Tu-bo*, another branch for An-xi. There were also 13 tribes that were close to the khan court and had accepted Wu-jie the *Te-qin* as their khan; they headed south and became subjects of the Han Chinese."[160] (The *Ge-luo-lu* are the Karluks; the *Tu-bo* are the Tibetans; *An-xi* means Protectorate General to Pacify the West; and *Te-qin* i.e., *Tegin* means commander or prince.[161]) Of these,

---

[159] Lu Simian, *History of Sui, Tang and Five Dynasties,* vol. I (*Sui-tang-wu-dai-shi*, Beijing: China Friendship Publishing Company, 2009), 318. （吕思勉：《隋唐五代史》）

[160] Liu, *OBoT*, "Uyghurs", 3547. "有回鹘相馺职者，拥外甥庞特勤及男鹿并遏粉等兄弟五人、一十五部西奔葛逻禄，一支投吐蕃，一支投安西，又有近可汗牙十三部，以特勤乌介为可汗，南来附汉。"

[161] Shang, "An Initial Probing into the Political System of Ancient

the southbound Uyghurs entered the territory of Tang China, with more than half of them settling down in the area of present-day Shanxi province. Other than a small group that stayed behind in the *Gan-zhou* and the Khara-Khoto area in Gansu province and western Inner Mongolia) and that were historically known as the *Gan-zhou* Uyghurs, whose state lasted until 1028,[162] the rest of the 15 Uyghur tribes comprising about 100 thousand people who made up the main Uyghur force headed west under the leadership of Pang the *Tegin* (that is, the aforementioned *Pang-te-qin*), and came to the Xinjiang area of *Gu-cheng* (also called *Bei-ting*, present-day Jimsar, which is east of present-day Urumqi) and Kocho (*Gao-chang*; also called *Xi-zhou*, near present-day Turpan).[163]

In 842 and 843, ten of the thirteen tribes that followed the 14th Uyghur khan, Uge (Wu-jie), surrendered to and became part of Tang China, while two tribes "sought shelter west with the Tibetans", meaning they joined the *Gan-zhou* Uyghurs. The last tribe sought shelter with the great *Shi-wei* people in the northeastern steppes.[164] Uge

---

Uighur Khanate in Northern Mongolia", citing 15.

[162] Liu, *OBoT*, "Uyghurs", 3547; Li, *Xinjiang*, 43-44.

[163] Liu, *OBoT*, "Uyghurs", 3547; Li, *Xinjiang*, 45.

[164] Li, *Xinjiang,* 42-43; Liu, *OBoT*, "Uyghurs", 3547-3548. Note that the *OBoT* says 13 tribes followed Uge Khan, but its list of all the tribes totals 14, including two tribes that sought shelter with the *Shi-wei*. Therefore, if 13 is accurate for the total number of tribes, then the number of tribes that sought shelter with the *Shi-wei* might have only

Khan was killed by Uyghur aristocrats. According to the *OBoT*, "The people led by Uge Khan surrendered in the first year of the *Da-zhong* reign in the *You-zhou* region. Aimless wandering, starvation and freezing temperatures had reduced the hundred thousand people to fewer than 3,000."[165] (The first year of the *Da-zhong* is 847, *You-zhou* is the Beijing area.) In the spring of the second year of the *Da-zhong* reign, the last of the khans, E-nian Khan, and "nine others rode west on horseback" and disappeared. The Khyagas captured all the remnants of the Uyghurs living with the *Shi-wei* and brought them back north.[166] Therefore, we can conclude that it was the year **848** that marked the complete destruction of the Uyghur regime on the steppes. This was a highly significant year for China: it was the definitive conclusion to a millennium of threats and wars from the Huns in the north and their Tlughish (*Te-le*-ish) descendants that began in the Han dynasty. However, in close succession, the Khitans and the *Jin* (Aisin) subsequently emerged on the grasslands to become even more powerful enemies of China.

Among the westbound Uyghurs was another group that continued west, cutting across the Ili River and Issyk-Kul Lake basin in the western part of the Tianshan

---

been one tribe, not two.

[165] Liu, *OBoT*, "Uyghurs", 3548. "乌介部众至大中元年诣幽州降，留者漂流饿冻，众十万，所存止三千已下。"

[166] Liu, *OBoT*, "Uyghurs", 3548. "……等九骑西走，……"

mountain range, then moving south until they arrived in an area south of the Karluk Khanate and entering the grasslands west of the Pamir Mountains. They remained under Pang's khanate for some years, but later established the Kara-Khanid Khanate (kara or *ka-la* means "black", but here the translation should be "big" or "great") principally between the Amu Darya and Syr Darya rivers. Its ruling center was initially Balasagun (present-day Tokmok, Kyrgyzstan) and later Kashgar.[167] This newly established kingdom ultimately became Uzbekistan. The majority of the Uyghurs, however, stayed in Xinjiang's northeast and south and became the Kocho Uyghur Khanate. Pang the *Tegin* became the khan of Kocho Khanate with the title of Kun Tengride Qut Bolmish Kuchluk Bilga Khan. By his use of "Bilga", he showed that his khanate was the legitimate continuation of the Uyghur Khanate of the East Asian steppes.

A branch of the west migrated Uyghurs, relatively small in number, entered the *He-xi* Corridor (that is, the corridor west of the Yellow River) in present-day Gansu province, and in 860 or 866 became established in *Gan-zhou*.[168] The *Old History of the Five Dynasties* says: "The rest of them went west and became the subjects of the *Tu-bo, Gan-zhou* is located in *Tu-bo*."[169] (*Gan-zhou* was later

---

[167] Li, *Xinjiang*, 47-48.

[168] Grousset, *Empire,* 125.

[169] Li, *Xinjiang*, 43; Xue, *Old History of the Five Dynasties,*

called *Kang-zhou* and is today the city of Zhangye.) *Tu-bo* is Tibet, and at this time, Tibetans controlled the region between China and the Western Regions. These Uyghurs were known as the *Gan-zhou* Uyghurs and they were later joined by some Uyghurs who had tried unsuccessfully to migrate south. They defeated and expelled the Tibetans a decade after they migrated here. The *Gan-zhou* or *He-xi* Uyghurs later were called the *Gan-zhou-Sha-zhou* Uyghurs because their khanate expanded to include *Sha-zhou* (Dunhuang), in 980 at the latest, according to the *History of Song*.[170]

The *Gan-zhou* Uyghurs maintained contact with the Uyghurs that had migrated south and west, and they mutually supported each other. They also maintained friendly relations with China. For instance, in 980, their Khan Yaghlaqar Bilga, who had the same tribal name as the founding khan of the Orkhon khanate established on the steppes in 744, sent a tribute-bearing delegation to the

---

"Uyghurs", 1276-1277. "馀众西奔，归于吐蕃，吐蕃处之甘州。"

[170] Tuo-tuo (Toqtoa), *History of Song*, Chronicle 249, Foreign Nations VI, "Uyghurs" (Beijing: Zhonghua Book Company, 2000), 10890-10891. "In the fifth year [of the *Tai-ping-xing-guo* reign (980)], the *Gan-Sha-zhou* Uyghur khan Yaghlaqhr Bilga sent envoys Pei Yi and three others to China's Song dynasty with gifts of one-humped camels, famous horses, coral and amber." "五年，甘、沙州回鹘可汗夜落纥密礼遏遣使裴溢的等四人，以橐驼、名马、珊瑚、琥珀来献。" (脱脱：《宋史》)

court of China's Song dynasty.[171] In 1028, the *Gan-zhou* Uyghur Khanate was defeated by the Western Xia kingdom's Tangut people.[172] One group of the Uyghur survivors, called "*Huang-tou* Uyghurs" (which means blonde Uyghurs) in Song China history books[173] fled in 1081 to Qiemo County in present-day Xinjiang after which they might have become *Sha-zhou* Uyghurs.[174] During the Mongol Empire, they were also called Sari Uyghurs (Sari means yellow) in Chinese historical texts,[175] and in the early 15th century they migrated back to *Gan-zhou*.[176] A different view of the Sari Uyghurs, with which I disagree, says they probably belonged to the Kocho Uyghur branch.[177]

In this way, the ancestors of the Uyghurs completed the transition from a nomadic to a sedentary lifestyle, which they have maintained to this day. Today, the descendants of the Uyghurs in Gansu province are known

---

[171] Cheng Suluo, *Collection of History of the Tang and Song Dynasties on Uyghurs* (Beijing: People's Publishing House, 1994), 144. (程溯洛：《唐宋回鹘史论集》）

[172] Grousset, *Empire,* 125.

[173] Tuo-tuo, *History of Song*, Foreign Nations VI, "Khotan" (*Yu-tian*), 10887.

[174] Li, *Xinjiang,* 44-45.

[175] Song, *History of Yuan*, Chronicle 8, *Su-bu-tai*, 1966; Grousset, *Empire,* 125.

[176] Li, *Xinjiang,* 45.

[177] Li, *Xinjiang,* 45.

as the Yugurs (close in pronunciation to Uyghur).[178] The Uyghurs who migrated south, living in present-day Shanxi province, were later called the *Wang-gu* (Onguds) during the Mongol Empire. They will be mentioned later in this thesis because some of them played important roles, both religiously and politically, in the history of Euro-Asian diplomatic activities.

The majority of the Uyghurs migrated west however and settled in Xinjiang's northeast and south.

4. The Independent Kocho Khanate Uyghurs (841–1130): the origin of Uyghuristan and the modern Uyghur identity

Before the fall of their khanate in 841, the Uyghur military and administrative forces had already penetrated deep into the Xinjiang region for nearly a century, mainly around the northeastern rim of the Tarim Basin and centered around the areas of *Bei-ting* and Kocho, where the Red *Di* people's *Gao-che* Kingdom used to stand three centuries ago, the key hub areas of the Silk Road connecting China and the West Regions. So, when approximately one-third of the Uyghurs who moved west under the leadership of Pang the *Tegin* settled here, it was not an aimless exile. **First,** after several decades of

---

[178] Li, *Xinjiang*, 45.

military campaigns, the Orkhon Uyghurs finally succeeded in 792 in wresting complete control of the city from the hands of the Karluks, Basmyls, and Tibetans, Beshbalik (*Bei-ting*, Jimsar) at the north of the Tianshan mountain range, the strategic town of the Silk Road, and continued to hold it until the fall of the Orkhon Khanate.[179] **Second,** history has proven how correct this choice was, and later events showed that whether it was the Uyghurs who moved south or other branches of the Uyghurs who moved to the near west or the far west, they all either disappeared into history or became largely Turkified. Only the Kocho Uyghurs survived with a relatively pure bloodline and the title of "Uyghur", to become the symbolic antecedents of the later Uyghuristan and the symbolic forefathers of the modern Uyghurs.[180] To be more inclusive, as James Millward pointed out: "Russian Orientalist scholars in the late nineteenth century had proposed that the Muslim inhabitants of the Xinjiang oases were Uyghur by virtue of descent from the Turfan Uyghur kingdom and the Qarahahanids."[181] Here the Qarahahanids evidently referred to those who were in the Kashgar region, which used to be part of the Kocho Uyghur Khanate originally.

In 842, the Khyagas (Kyrgyz), who had still not given up on attacking the Uyghurs, set upon them from the

---

[179] Clark, "Bügü Khan", 107.

[180] Millward, *Crossroads*, 52.

[181] Millward, *Crossroads*, 208.

western part of the Mongolian grasslands. They occupied *Bei-ting* and Kocho, forcing Pang the *Tegin* to retreat west to Karasahr (*Yan-qi*, Arshi).[182] At this time and place, Pang the *Tegin* declared himself *Yabghu* (a princely or viceroy title in the *Yue-zhi* tradition that was used by the Kushan kingdom and later by the Turks and Uyghurs) to show that he still recognized the khanship of the Uge Khan who was still wandering about the southern part of the Mongolian grasslands close to the Chinese border.[183] Beginning in 843, the Uyghurs began to settle around the both sides of the eastern Tianshan mountain range including around the oases along the northeastern rim of the Tarim Basin.[184] In 848, when the Khyagas carried off the Uyghur remnants, including the high-ranking officials and aristocracy, to the north, "Pang the *Tegin* proclaimed himself khan over all the cities west of the desert. His descendants had weak kings and powerful ministers. Living in *Gan-zhou*, they did not enjoy the same prosperity as in olden times."[185] Pang the *Yabghu* became khan; his reign name was Kun Tengride Qut Bolmish Kuchluk Bilga Khan. The desert referred to in the quote is the *Ha-shun* Desert situated between Kumul (Hami in Xinjiang) and *Gan-zhou–Sha-zhou* (present-day Dunhuang

---

[182] Li, *Xinjiang*, 45-46.

[183] Li, *Xinjiang*, 45-46.

[184] Grousset, *Empire*, 125.

[185] Liu, *OBoT,* "Uyghurs", 3548-3549. "庞勒已自称可汗，有碛西诸城。其后嗣君弱臣强，居甘州，无复昔时之盛。"

in Gansu province). "West of the desert" refers to the area of present-day Turpan and Urumqi. At that time, some Uyghur remnants still remained on the steppes. According to Chinese the *OBoT*: "A few tents were still left on the other side of the Great Wall, spread out across the mountains and deep into the forests. [The people] stole and robbed from other ethnic groups, and they all looked toward the west eagerly awaiting Pang the *Tegin*'s arrival."[186]

Therefore, the area around the eastern Tianshan mountain range and the northeastern edge of the Tarim Basin became the center of activity for the Uyghurs led by Pang, the self-proclaimed khan. The Chinese Tang dynasty court conferred upon him the title of *Huai-jian* khan, thus recognizing the Uyghur Khanate's relocation to southwest of the Tang capital of Chang'an.[187]

According to the *Collection of Tang Dynasty Imperial Edicts and Orders* and the *Comprehensive Mirror in Aid of Governance*, in the early spring of 856 (the 10th year of the *Da-zhong* reign), Uyghur envoys arrived in Chang'an by way of the Chinese commandery of *Shuo-fang* (*Ling-wu*, at present-day Ningxia province). Other Uyghur emissaries traveling with the Khyagas envoy Li Jian also arrived in Chang'an. This was how the Tang court learned

---

[186] Li, *Xinjiang*, 45-46, 3548. "在外犹数帐，散藏诸山深林，盗劫诸蕃，皆西向倾心望安西庞勒之到。"

[187] Li, *Xinjiang*, 46.

that Pang the *Tegin* of the westward-migrating Uyghurs had already been declared khan. So the Tang emperor Xuan-zong issued the "Edict of Proposal to Establish the Uyghur Khan", which said that Chinese messengers were being sent to convey greetings advising the Uyghurs to return to their former homeland and royal court, and then conferred the title of khan upon Pang.[188] The emperor also stressed in the edict that China's Tang China would treat the Uyghur khan well, just as China's Han dynasty had treated the Hun *chan-yu* (that is, king) well, even though the *chan-yu* had harbored enmity for the Chinese, saying that the edict "re-establishes the former friendship, fulfills a good plan, and declares to the world that all might know my intentions".[189]

However, a November entry that same year in the *Collection of Tang Dynasty Imperial Edicts and Orders* says that upon arrival in *Ling-wu*, the Tang Chinese envoy unexpectedly met up with an emissary sent by the Uyghurs

---

[188] Song Min-qiu, *Collection of Tang Dynasty Imperial Edicts and Orders* (*Tang-da-zhao-ling-ji*, Song China: 1070), vol. 128 (Beijing: Commercial Press, 1959), 693 （宋敏求：《唐大诏令集》）; Si-ma, *Aid of Governance*, vol. 249, "Tang-ji 65", 8059; Rong Xinjiang, "New Evidence on the Tang Envoy to the Western Uighur Kingdom in 856", *Dunhuang Research*, No. 3. 2013, total No. 139 (Gansu: 2013), 128-132, citing 129-130. （荣新江：《大中十年唐朝遣使册立回鹘史事新证》，刊登于《敦煌研究》）

[189] Song, *Tang Dynasty Imperial Edicts*, Vol. 128, 693. "再寻旧好，意举良图，报告天下，咸知朕意。"

and together they went back to Chang'an.[190] This Uyghur envoy gave a full account to the Tang court of why the Uyghurs were not willing to return to their homeland north of the Great Wall, and explained that as strangers newly arrived in the Western Regions and "not having gained the trust of the surrounding ethnic groups and kingdoms, and worried that [you] suspect us of establishing a new kingdom, we send a special envoy in compliance with the ritualistic protocol for conferring the title."[191] That is, the westward-migrating Uyghurs wanted to get the Tang China to confer a title to its khan, which would help it win recognition from the various ethnic groups of the Western Regions while at the same time dispelling any fears within the Tang court that they were trying to set up a new kingdom in the Tang China's former sphere of colonial influence and therefore giving the Tang China no cause for concern.

According to the same entry, Tang China conferred the title of khan on Pang, who had previously been known as Pang the *Tegin* and then as Pang the *Yabghu*. The royal edict of this event first reviewed the friendship and diplomatic relations between the two states: "Since the establishment of their [Uyghur] kingdom, they have endeavored to be loyal and sincere, as in the relationship

---

[190] Si-ma, *Aid of Governance*, vol. 249, "Tang-ji 65", 8061.

[191] Si-ma, *Aid of Governance*, vol. 249, "Tang-ji 65", 8061. "尚恐未为诸蕃所信，犹疑新造之邦，是用特命使臣，遵行册礼。"

of a nephew with his uncle, communicating every year, with sincerity and with no suspicions, for the sake of both our nations."[192] Nevertheless, the edict still encouraged the Uyghur aristocracy to resolve to return to the Mongolian grasslands and restore their kingdom there. Lastly, the edict proclaimed the appointment of Wang Rui-zhang and Li Xun as the envoy and deputy envoy, respectively, to carry the royal edict to Pang conferring upon him the title Ulug Tengride Qut Bulmish alp Kulug Bilga Khan; in Chinese, Huai-jian Khan.[193] Thus, Pang became the legitimate khan in the traditional symbolic way. The November 856 entry in the *Collection of Tang Dynasty Imperial Edicts and Orders* says that this occurred in 857 (the 11th year of the *Da-zhong* reign), which is an obvious error. A contemporary Chinese scholar compared this account with the record in the *Comprehensive Mirror in Aid of Governance* concluded that the year 857 is wrong and should be 856 (the 10th year of the *Da-zhong* reign).[194] I agree with him.

This edict provides some valuable information and details that help us understand the sense of identity of the westward-migrating Uyghurs. From the title that was

---

[192] Song, *Tang Dynasty Imperial Edicts*, vol. 129, 698. "立国以来，尝效诚节，代为甥舅，每岁通和，推诚不疑，为我与国。"

[193] Song, *Tang Dynasty Imperial Edicts*, vol. 129, 698. 九姓回鹘嗢禄登里罗汩没密施合俱录毗伽怀建可汗

[194] Rong, "Tang Envoy", citing 130, footnote 1.

conferred on this khan, we can see that it continues to use the "Bilga Khan" title from their time as a kingdom on the grasslands. That is to say, the westward-migrating Uyghurs had not in fact established a new kingdom; rather, Pang became the legitimate successor to the Bilga Khan title, and this was acknowledged by Tang China's conferring of the title on him. In addition, they continued the good tradition of maintaining good relations with Tang China. In the *NBoT*, it says that after the title was conferred, the khanate of these westward-migrating Uyghurs "for more than a decade, always came to make tribute with their local gifts".[195]

In 863, the Khyagas (Kyrgyz) sent an envoy to the Tang court, asking for permission to attack the Uyghurs again and win back the *An-xi* region (*An-xi* is the Protectorate General to Pacify the West), which they would dedicate to Tang China. But the Tang court refused.[196] Clearly, Tang China abided by its long-standing treaty with its Uyghur allies. Note that as khan, Pang represented all the Uyghurs of the *An-xi* region, including all the Uyghur tribes in the entire Xinjiang region and the Uyghur tribes that had sought refuge with

---

[195] Ou-yang, *NBoT*, "Uyghurs II", 4664. "后十余年，一再献方物。"

[196] Si-ma: *Aid of Governance*, vol. 250, "Records of Tang 66", 8107. It says: "The Kyrgyzs wanted to attack the Uyghurs again and to present the whole of the Western Regions to Tang [China], but [Tang China] did not allow this." "黠戛斯遣其臣合伊难支表求经籍及每年遣使走马请历，又欲讨回鹘，使安西以来悉归唐，不许。"

the Karluks west of the Pamir Mountains. Note also that the *He-xi* Uyghurs and the southward-migrating Uyghurs were not part of this khanate. The possible reason will be explored in the final section of this chapter.

According to the *Comprehensive Mirror in Aid of Governance*, in 866, "The military governor Zhang Yi-chao, who switched his allegiance to the Tang, reported: the Uyghur Gu-jun from *Bei-ting* has occupied *Xi-zhou*, *Lun-tai*, *Qing-zhen* and other cities." [197] (*Xi-zhou* is Kocho.) This Zhang Yi-chao was originally the governor of *Sha-zhou* (Dunhuang), had served the Tibetans (*Tu-bo*), and in 851 successfully led an uprising of the local Chinese against the Tibetans and transferred their allegiance to Tang China, for which he was awarded a title. The Uyghur general Gu-jun served Zhang Yi-chao and continued attacking the Tibetans in the eastern parts of Xinjiang. The *Institutional History of Tang* says, "In the tenth month of the seventh year of the *Xian-tong* reign, the military governor of *Sha-zhou* Zhang Yi-chao reported [to the Tang court] that he had sent Uyghur chief Pu-gu-jun to engage Tibetan general Shang-kong-re in battle. The Tibetan enemies were soundly defeated, Shang-kong-re was executed, and his head was sent to the [Tang] court." [198] That was how Tang China finally saw the

---

[197] Si-ma: *Aid of Governance*, vol. 250, "Records of Tang 66", 8113.

[198] Wang Pu, *Institutional History of Tang* (*Tang-hui-yao*, 961), vol. 97, *Tubo* (Tibet) (Beijing: Zhonghua Book Company, 1955), 1741-

expulsion of the Tibetans and regained control of the portion of the Silk Road in the eastern part of the Tianshan mountain range, thereby re-establishing direct communication with *An-xi* (the Xinjiang region).

Thereafter, in 866 the Uyghur chief from *Bei-ting*, Pu-gu-jun, marched into Karasahr, killed the *Hui-jian* Khan, declared himself khan, and established *Bei-ting* as the capital. His successors later made Kocho a capital as well.[199] This was when the real sense of the khanate of the Kocho Uyghurs began to come into being. Note that the Kocho Uyghurs included all the Uyghurs in the area of the Tarim Basin, Kocho basin and present-day Urumqi. Afterward, the three branches of the westbound Uyghurs separated politically and became three different khanates.

According to the practice of Chinese historians, the westward-migrating Uyghurs are called the Western Uyghur Khanate [200] or the Later Uyghur Khanate,[201] because from a geographic standpoint they are situated west of their former khanate on the Mongolian steppes. Modern Chinese scholars also call it the *Xi-zhou* (which

---

1742. "咸通七年十月。沙州节度使张义潮奏。差回鹘首领仆固俊与吐蕃大将尚恐热交战。大败蕃寇。斩尚恐热。传首京师。"
（王溥：《唐会要》）

[199] Li, *Xinjiang*, 46.

[200] Li, *Xinjiang*, 46.

[201] As the Eastern Turkic Khanate is also called the Second Turkic Khanate or the Later Turkic Khanate.

means "western prefecture", i. e. Kocho) Uyghur kingdom.[202] Modern Western-Russian scholars introduced the terms "West Turkestan" and "East Turkestan". The Russian sinologist Nikita Bichurin first used these terms in 1829 writing that 'it would be better here to call Bukhara's Turkestan the Western one, and Chinese Turkestan the Eastern [...] The name "Chinese Turkestan" should be changed.' (1829, 12),'[203] with other Western writers and politicians following suit. These new terms were employed primarily to differentiate the ancient Uzbekistan-based Uyghur Kara-Khanid Khanate that was established west of the Pamir Mountains from the Kocho Uyghur Khanate east of the Pamir Mountains. The term "East Turkestan" or "Eastern Turkestan" has ever since affected or confused the "sense of direction" of modern scholars as well as of modern Uyghurs with regard to the geographic attribute of the Uyghur identity, together with the sacrifice of their ethnic attribute being Turkified.

In this thesis, I decided to call the three West migrated Uyghurs as Later Uyghur Khanate before their political separations. After their political separations, I called Kara-

---

[202] Gao Yongjiu, *General Study on Ancient Ethnic Religions of the Western Regions* (Beijing: Higher Education Press, 1997), 219. （高永久：《西域古代民族宗教论》）

[203] Kamalov, "Soviet Historiography on the Uyghurs", citing 33–34. East Turkestan was also called Chinese Turkestan in comparison to Russian Turkestan, i.e., the West Turkestan taken over by Russia in 1867.

Khanid Khanate the Western Uyghur Khanate, the Kocho Uyghur Khanate the Eastern Uyghur Khanate, and the Uyghurs in *Gan-zhou* and *Sha-zhou* the Sari Uyghur Khanate. I called the South migrated Uyghurs at the northern board of China the *Wang-gu* (Ongud) Uyghur kingdom.

Thereafter, mention of the Uyghurs in Chinese histories dropped sharply. The *Comprehensive Mirror in Aid of Governance* explained, "Later their [Uyghur] court was chaotic, so their tributes did not come [to China] regularly and [our] history book lost track of them."[204] In 901, Tang China experienced internal chaos and the emperor Zhao-zong was abducted by the court eunuch Han Quan-hui to Fengxiang, Shaanxi province.[205] In 902, at this calamitous time for the Tang, the "Uyghurs sent an envoy bearing gifts and offered to send troops to help overcome the crisis".[206] But Emperor Zhao-zong and his minister were wary and answered the Uyghur khan with a

---

[204] Si-ma's *Aid of Governance*, quoted in Lu, *Sui, Tang and Five Dynasties*, 318.

[205] Si-ma, *Aid of Governance*, vol. 262, "Records of Tang 78", 8559; Ou-yang, *NBoT*, "Uyghurs II", 4464.

[206] Si-ma, *Aid of Governance*, vol. 263, "Records of Tang 79", 8573: "回鹘遣使入贡，请发兵赴难"; Ou-yang, *NBoT*, "Uyghurs II", 4664, it says: "When the [Tang] emperor Zhao-zong was in *Feng-xiang*, the military governor of *Ling-zhou*, Han Xun, told him that the Uyghurs had asked for permission to send their troops to help [Tang] in its crisis." "昭宗幸凤翔，灵州节度使韩逊表回鹘请率兵赴难。"

polite refusal. Five years later, the Tang dynasty was destroyed, and China fell into chaos. It would be 981, in the early Song dynasty, before the Kocho Uyghurs would reappear in the Chinese history books and the two kingdoms would resume diplomatic contacts. The *Ganzhou* Uyghurs first re-appeared in Chinese history books with the rise of the Khitans. According to the *History of Liao*, in 924, when the Khitan khan Abaoji, founder of the Liao Kingdom, led his troops to conquer the eastern part of the Tianshan mountain range, he "took captive the governor of *Gan-zhou* governor, *Bi-li-e*, so [Abaoji] sent an envoy to his lord, Khan Ormuzd".[207]

In this way, the ancestors of today's Uyghurs completed their transition from a nomadic life to the settled lifestyle they still follow today. In the process, the Kocho Uyghurs also completed the Hunnic-Uyghurization of Xinjiang through Uyghurizing the eastern part of the Tarim Basin and the Kocho-*Bei-ting* region.[208] This was a watershed moment in the history of the civilizations of Central Asia. It also firmly fixed Xinjiang as the symbolic representation of the geographic attribute of the Uyghur identity. The *An-xi* Uyghurs, or later the well-known Kocho Uyghurs, have lived in Xinjiang ever since, right

---

[207] Tuo-tuo (Toqtoa), *History of Liao* (*Liao-shi*, 1343), Ben-ji II, "The Founding Emperor II" (Beijing: Zhonghua Book Company, 2000), 14. "获甘州回鹘都督毕离遏，因遣使谕其主乌母主可汗。"（脱脱：《辽史》）

[208] Grousset, *Empire*, 125.

up to the present day, a span of 1,100 years. In this respect, the fact that the Uyghur people from this point on looked upon Xinjiang as their own territory is justifiable. The Uyghurs west of the Pamir Mountains at last became the Uzbeks who basically maintain the same Uyghur language yet with a slightly harsher sound because it "lacks the vowel harmony".[209] Uzbeks now live mainly in Uzbekistan and other countries bordering Xinjiang.

According to the research of the prominent contemporary ethnic historian Cheng Suluo, which combined Chinese, the Uyghur-language of the Kocho Uyghurs, and Persian historical materials, the territory of the Kocho Uyghur Khanate had Hami as its eastern border, stretched west to *Bing-da-ban* of the Tianshan mountain range on the northern side of Aksu, adjoined Yutian-Turpan in the south, and reached the Ili River in the north.[210] This would have been the boundaries of the Kocho Khanate from the mid-9th century to the 11th century. In 1006, the Muslims of the Kara-Khanid Khanate occupied Yu-tian. Note how surprisingly vast was

---

[209] Richard Schafer, *A Muslim Became A Christian*, translated from German to English by John Bechard, (England: Author Online Ltd., 2002), 79-80.

[210] Cheng Suluo, "Critical Analysis on History of Song: Gang-chang Chronicle", Luo Bingliang (ed.), *Research on History of Song* (Beijing: Encyclopedia of China Publishing House, 2009), 372-404, citing 384. [程溯洛：" 《宋史•高昌传》笺证"，出自罗炳良（分卷主编）的《宋史研究》]

the extent of the power of the Kocho Uyghur Khanate, extending north as far as the Ili River. The *Compendium of the Languages of the Turks* from the 1070s corroborates this, saying, "We crossed the waters of Ili by boat (this is a wide river), headed in the direction of the Uyghur people, and we captured Minglak (the Uyghur kingdom)."[211] The *Boundaries of the World* tells us that the king of the Yagma people was of the same clan of the Kocho Uyghurs, but according to the research of Russian scholar of Central Asia V. Berthold, the Yagma people were a nomadic, militaristic tribe of the Nine Surnames Uyghurs that had occupied Kashgar prior to 940, and in 940 occupied the Zhetysu region.[212] So as the territory of the Kocho Uyghurs, the Ili River valley was likely the territory of and settled mainly also by the Yagma-Uyghur people, even though in the mid-8th century the Yagma had been driven out by the westward military campaign of the Uyghur kingdom from the steppes.

It is my view that the Yagma people, although a separate tribe, were subjugated by the Uyghurs, similar to the way the *Tele*-Uyghurs had been subjugated by and served as a military tribe to the Turks but were not the same ethnic group; they simply had mutually comprehensible spoken languages and similar customs,

---

[211] Mahmud Kashgari, *Compendium of the Languages of the Turks*, vol. 3 (Beijing: Publishing House of Minority Nationalities, 2002), 231.（麻赫默德•喀什噶里：《突厥语大词典》）

[212] Cheng, "Gao-chang Chronicle", citing 392-393.

and politically were part of the Kocho Uyghur khanate, just like the *Wu-sun* people who had acted as the troops for the military campaigns of the Hun *Chan-yu*, driving out the Greater *Yue-zh*i people and occupying the Zhetysu region. Similar to the Yagmas, the leader of the Basmyls tribe was, as was also mentioned earlier, from the Turkic royal Ashina clan, yet he still launched a joint Uyghur-Basmyl revolution that overthrew the Turk's Khanate.

In short, the period around 940 was when the territory of the Kocho Uyghurs was the most expansive, basically controlling both the northern and southern branches of the Silk Road in the Xinjiang region including Ili and Kashgar to the west, therefore covering roughly the same areas as the entire Xinjiang territory occupied in 1759 by the Manchu Qing dynasty. However, after 960 when the Kashgar (Kara-Khanid) Uyghurs converted to Islam, the territory of the Kocho Uyghur Khanate shrank because of the *jihad* against the infidel Kocho Uyghurs by the Kara-Khanid Khanate after it converted to Islam. Based on the above references from the *Compendium of the Languages of the Turks* and other sources, it appears that the first territory lost by the Kocho Uyghur khanate was the region of Kashgar before 960 and the region of Ili after 960. By the time of Chenghis Khan's conquests in the 13th century, the Kocho Uyghur Khanate had basically been reduced to its 841 territory after the Uyghurs' westward migration.

Finally, people generally regard the Uyghurs and other Turkic speaking peoples as the original inhabitants of Xinjiang and Central Asia, and the Uyghurs thus also view Xinjiang as the inalienable geographical attribute of their ethnic identity; this view of their identity's geographic attribute includes some understandable historical misunderstandings. In fact, though, before the Uyghurs moved west and occupied Xinjiang and part of Central Asia, the natives of another racial group had already been living in this region for about 2,600 years. It is they who are the original inhabitants, in the real sense of the word. The linguists called them Indo-Europeans, and I call them White Indo-Europeans.

The earliest inhabitants of North Central Asia and North Xinjiang were Scythians. Historians believe they were Iranian, a conclusion based mostly on information about their language and customs. But the factual evidence found in the Chinese classics shows that they were the same type of people as Mediterranean Southern Europeans and that this is why they appear to have some of the characteristics of modern-day Iranians. Therefore, I call them Scythian Indo-Europeans. Because the Chinese Han dynasty classic *Book of Han* called them Saka people (*Sai-ren*) or Saka race (*Sai-zhong*),[213] I also call them Scythian-

---

[213] Ban, *Book of Han*, Chronicle 66 I, "Western Regions" (Beijing: Zhonghua Book Company, 1999), 2863. It says: "The Saka race is spread out, often splitting up and establishing different kingdoms. Northwest of *Shu-le* are *Xiu-xun* and *Yuan-du*, in ancient times they all

Saka people. As for the Sogdian region and the Tarim Basin, similar evidence from the Chinese classics show that the earliest inhabitants were Aryans, so I call them Aryan Indo-Europeans, which includes the Khyagas people who were first Hunnified and later Tlughurized to become the Kyrkyz at last. Some ancient Chinese history books say they are a branch of the Saka people, but starting in the Tang dynasty they were called the *Hu* people, so I also call them the Aryan-*Hu* people.

Another name for both groups who were living on the East Asian steppes is North Asian whites, who were called *Northern Di* which includes *Red Di* (such as Scythian *Gao-che* people) and *White Di* (such as Aryan Khyagas) in the Chinese classics, this being suitable.

II. Clarifying the Difference between the Uyghurs and the People of Turkey

Many Uyghurs today, intentionally or not, are trying to identify themselves with Turkey. This has resulted in the common misconception among the Han-Chinese that the Uyghurs are Turkish and want to establish an "East Turkey-stan" and that they call themselves "people of East Turkey" rather than the fact that they want to reestablish "East Turkestan". Meanwhile, some Uyghur intellectuals

---

belonged to the Saka race."

nowadays have gone to study at the University of Turkey in hopes of finding a way to reinvigorate the Uyghurs and to seek political independence for the Uyghurs. Over the past 20 years, Turkey has become, in the minds of the Uyghurs, a politically sacred land of an advanced Turkic civilization with Islam as its attribute.

Indirect political contact between Xinjiang's Uyghurs and Ottoman Turkey began in the late 19th century afer Yaqub Beg, the leader of a rebellion in Xinjiang that was put down by Qing dynasty China, his "fallen emirate" fled to Turkey and was granted asylum by Istanbul.[214] At that time, the indirect religious influence of Istanbul on Xinjiang was also starting to become apparent as the Turkish capital city served as a transit point for Xinjiang Muslims on their pilgrimage to Mecca.[215] At the beginning of the 20th century, because the New Method Schools established in Xinjiang as part of the Jadidist movement took the initiative in learning from and adopting the Ottoman Turkish educational system, Istanbul's political-religious ideology impacted a generation of Uyghur intellectuals, just as China's New Culture Movement, meanwhile, was indoctrinating a generation of Han-Chinese intellectuals with the Soviet Union's Communist political ideology.

---

[214] Brophy, *Uyghur Nation*, 87.

[215] Brophy, *Uyghur Nation*, 87.

Because of the dominant effect of Turkification through aggressive Islamification that began long ago in history, the Uyghurs gradually lost their knowledge and memory of their own original ethnic name that was associated with the Orkhon Khanate and its successor, the Kocho Khanate, and later Uyghuristan. In its stead, ironically, they accepted the appellation "Turk" and "Turki", the ethnic name of their ancestors' longtime enemy. Before 1949, non-Chinese materials universally referred to Xinjiang as "Chinese Turkestan" or "East Turkestan". In 1933-1934 when Uyghurs in Kashgar established the "Turkic Islamic Republic of East Turkestan", sometimes shortened to the "Eastern Turkestan Republic", "the new government struck its first copper coins in the name of the "Republic of Uyhuristan" (*Uyghuristan Jumhuriyiti*), but later coins and passports were labeled 'Eastern Turkestan Republic'."[216] The reason for the name change from Uyghuristan to Turkestan was to include Xinjiang's other Turkic speaking peoples.[217] The short-lived Uyghurs' sense of ethnic identity thus once again submitted to the rule of political ideology. In 1944-1945, Uyghurs in Ghuljia (Ili) established a second "Eastern Turkestan Republic" that still retained the Islamic and Turkified attributes.[218]

---

[216] Millward, *Crossroad*, 202-203.

[217] Millward, *Crossroad*, 203.

[218] Millward, *Crossroad*, 215-216.

A Brief Narrative of the Historical and Geographic Attributes of the Uyghur Identity

In order to understand the unique ethnic attribute of the Uyghurs, we must clarify the historical and ethnic attributes of the Turkish people, and then compare those with that of the Uyghurs, so as to prove that not only are the two essentially different despite some similarities, but that they are actually even more different than the Uyghurs were from the ancient Turks.

1. The origins and formation of Turkey

The word "*Uygar*" in the modern Turkish language means "civilized", which reveals the high esteem in which Turkey's people hold the Uyghur civilization.[219]

In the 10th century, in present-day Kyrgyzstan-Kazakhstan, that is the Ili River Valley-Lake Balkhash area, lived the Turkic tribe called the "Ghuzz", who were called Turkmen ("Our Turkomans") during the Chenghis Khan era.[220] Under the leadership of Seljuk, one branch of the Ghuzzs (the forefathers of modern Turkey) entered the Bukhara area (in present-day Uzbekistan) in 985, and took advantage of the destruction on October 23, 999, of the Islamic Samanid Empire of the Iranian people in the Transoxiana area by the Western Uyghur Kara-Khanid

---

[219] Rudelson, *Oasis Identities*, 31.

[220] Grousset, *Empire,* 148.

Khanate.²²¹ While the area was in a state of chaos, these Ghuzz entered the heartland of Transoxiana.²²² Around 1025, the leader of the Seljuk-Ghuzz people started to call himself *"yabghu"*,²²³ that is, the title first used by the *Yue-zhi* Kushan and later by the Turks and Uyghurs. During this period, they sided with the Kara-Khanids, holding back the Ghaznavids, another Turkic Islamic kingdom.²²⁴ What needs to be mentioned is that although Islam had long taken hold in Central Asia since 751, these Ghuzz seemed to be the exception, probably because at least some of them were Christians, which they remained until the Mongols took over the region in the early 13th century.

On May 22, 1040, near Merv (present-day in Turkmenistan), the Seljuk-Ghuzz people completely defeated the Ghaznavid Kingdom.²²⁵ In the 40 years that followed, these Turkic Ghuzz occupied Iraq and Western Persia, and started to assimilate with the Islamic culture, becoming the first sultanate recognized by both the Arabic caliph and the Sunni sect.²²⁶ In 1071, under the leadership of their sultan Alp Arslan (1063-1072), the Seljuk-Ghuzz people went to war in Malazgirt (historically called

---

²²¹ Grousset, *Empire*, 144.

²²² Grousset, *Empire*, 149.

²²³ Grousset, *Empire*, 149; the title is equivalent to Vice Khan (Geng, *Turkic Inscriptions,* 13).

²²⁴ Grousset, *Empire*, 149.

²²⁵ Grousset, *Empire*, 150.

²²⁶ Grousset, *Empire*, 151-152.

Manzikert, a city built by the Armenians, now a small town in the Turkish province of Mus) against troops led by the Byzantine emperor Romanos Diogenes; they thoroughly routed the Byzantines and captured their emperor.[227] Under the leadership of Alp Arslan's successor, Sultan Malishah (1072—1092), the Seljuk-Ghuzz people occupied Nicaea in Asia Minor in about 1081 (in present-day Turkey, the place where the Council of Nicaea was held).[228] In the 1070s and 1080s, they twice went on the offensive against the Kara-Khanid in the Transoxiana, forcing it into subjugation.[229] The Turks and the Uyghurs seemed to be continuing here the battles of their ancestors on the East Asia steppes going back to the 7th-8th century.

After all these wars, these Ghuzz people finally settled down in Asia Minor, where the natural surroundings made it seem like they had returned to their home, the Kyrgyz grasslands in the Ili River valley-Lake Balkhash area.[230] At the time, they occupied three territories: in Persia, the population was mainly still Iranian; in Syria, other than in the areas of Antioch and Alexandretta, the Ghuzz people lived scattered across the

---

[227] Grousset, *Empire*, 152.

[228] Grousset, *Empire*, 153.

[229] Grousset, *Empire*, 152-153.

[230] Grousset, *Empire*, 155.

land;[231] only in Asia Minor, on the Anatolian Plateau of the Byzantine Empire, did the Ghuzz supplant the Byzantine farmers and succeed in making the place thoroughly Turkic[232] and Islamic. In 1141, the Khitan people fleeing the Mongolian steppes and north China invaded and occupied Transoxiana and attacked and defeated the Persianized Seljuk-Ghuzz Sultanate; in 1153, the "Oghuz or Ghuzz, that is to say, people of the same ethnic stock as the Seljuks—from near Balkh" in present-day Afghanistan thoroughly defeated the Seljuk-Ghuzz people and the latter became what would later be known as Turkmenistan (Please note Grousset's uncertainty as to whether they were Oghuz or Ghuzz).[233] At the same time, the Seljuk-Ghuzz people on the Anatolian plateau, under the leadership of the Ghuzz Sultanate in Konya (present-day Konya, Turkey) and then later the Osman or Ottoman Empire (late 13th century to early 20th century), were ultimately thoroughly Turkified and Islamified all of the Byzantine lands of Asia Minor and became the forefathers of present-day Turkey.[234]

Over the course of the 11th century, the Ghuzz people who originated in Central Asia effected through large-scale immigration the swift Turkification and

---

[231] Grousset, *Empire,* 155.

[232] Grousset, *Empire,* 155, 157.

[233] Grousset, *Empire,* 159-160, 164.

[234] Grousset, *Empire,* 164.

Islamification of Western Asia. In 1071 or 1073, the ever more powerful and already Islamic Seljuk-Ghuzz captured Jerusalem from the hands of the Egyptians[235] and made it very hard or sometimes even impossible for Christians from other lands to come on pilgrimage to Jerusalem. In 1081, the Seljuk-Ghuzz founded its kingdom on the peninsula of Asia Minor in the eastern part of the Byzantine Empire.[236] All the Turkic Ghuzz tribes, including the Seljuk-Ghuzz, continued their never-ending conquests and expansion, transforming large swaths of Christian areas into territory under Islamic rule. This resulted in escalating feelings on the part of the Byzantine Empire and Europe, especially the Pope, of being encroached upon and threatened. Therefore, in March 1095, Byzantine Emperor Alexius appealed to the Pope to send troops to aid the Byzantine Empire and the Church of the East that were then being attacked and harassed for over two decades.[237] So the Western Roman Church planned and prepared to seize Jerusalem by military force. In the following 200-plus years, crusades were launched repeatedly. The first was sent by Pope Urban II in

---

[235] Muslim historical records differ as to the exact year; D. S. Richards (tr.), *The Annals of the Saljuq Turks: Selections from. al-Kamil fi'l-Ta'rikh of Ibn al-Athir* (New York: Routledge, 2002), 172 with footnote 42; 190.

[236] Richards (tr.), *The Annals of the Saljuq Turks*, 153.

[237] Jonathan Riley-Smith (ed.), *The Oxford History of the Crusades* (New York: Oxford University Press, 2002), 2.

November 1095 and captured Jerusalem in July 1099.[238] This First Crusade, which ended in 1102, had the "twin aims of freeing Christians from the yoke of Islamic rule and liberating the tomb of Christ, the Holy Sepulchre in Jerusalem, from Muslim control".[239]

Chenghis Khan conquered the Western Liao Kingdom in 1218, and in 1220 destroyed the Iranian-Turkic Muslim Khwarazmian kingdom. After occupying the entire Amu River area, Iraq, and East Persia, the Mongol Empire under the command of Ogedei Khan in the winter of 1230-1231 dispatched Chormaghan (or Chormaqan) *Noyan* (meaning military commander) to lead 30,000 troops to attack West Persia and try to restore the Khwarazmian prince Jalal ad-Din Mingburnu to the throne. They won a resounding victory, obtained possession of Persia, and stationed their troops in the Mugan and Arran plains for 10 years. In 1242, Chormaghan's successor, Baiju Noyan (commander 1242-1256), led the Mongol troops to attack Konya, the capital of the quite powerful and prosperous Seljuk Sultanate (ruled by Sultan Kai-Khosrau, 1237-1245), and occupy Erzurum; on June 26, 1243, in Kozadagh, near Erzincan,

---

[238] Riley-Smith (ed.), *The Oxford History of the Crusades*, 1, 2; Steven Runciman, *The First Crusade* (UK: Cambridge University Press, 1980), 187, 189.

[239] Riley-Smith (ed.), *The Oxford History of the Crusades*; Steven Runciman, *The First Crusade* (UK: Cambridge University Press, 1980), 187, 189.

they routed the Seljuk-Ghuzz army under the personal command of Sultan Kai-Khosrau. So, the Seljuk-Ghuzz sultanate surrendered and became a vassal state of the Mongol Empire. The iron hoof of the Mongols had now reached "the border of the Greek Empire".[240]

The Seljuk-Ghuzz in ancient Turkey were part of the ruling class, but their numbers were very small. As a result, their Turkic ethnicity mutated significantly to be "Turkish". In the Turkish sultanate at that time were many churches and Christians; the Christians were mainly Armenians and Greeks. This fact is documented in the travelogues of William of Rubruck, sent by the French King Louis IX to the Mongol Empire in 1253-1255. About the population of the Ghuzz Turks, he wrote: "Concerning Turkey, your Majesty shall understand, that the tenth man there, is not a Saracen: nay, they are all Armenians, and Greeks".[241] In the same way, the Turks in Central Asia-Xinjiang ruled the native white Indo-Europeans, who were the great majority, and through their initiating of the mixing of bloodlines and through cultural conquest, especially the later cultural conquest or even cultural genocide by Islam, they created a new identity and a new history for the natives and these regions. It appears that by

---

[240] Grousset, *Empire,* 261, 263.

[241] Vatch Ghazarian (ed.), *Armenians in the Ottoman Empire: An Anthology of Transformation 13th-19th Centuries* (Mayreni Publishing: Waltham, Massachusetts, 1997), 4-5.

immigrating to Europe, today's descendants of the Turks are perpetuating this same strategy.

According to the eyewitness accounts and travel diaries of non-Armenians from different periods of the Ottoman Empire, during the time of the Ottoman Empire, many Armenians converted to Islam due to direct or indirect government pressure. In fact, the main component of the Ottoman Empire population were children snatched from their Armenian and Greek Christian parents (and from the Jews and other ethnic groups) and then separated and isolated. Through systemized education aimed at Turkicization and training in the Islam faith, they grew up "Turkish". This was the method used to increase the numbers of "Turkish people" and reduce the number of Christian believers.[242]

One traveler in the 17th century, Paul Rycaut, wrote about this in a 1666 entry on the Turkish people: "...No people in the world have ever been more open to receive all sorts of nations to them, than they <the Turks>, nor have used more arts to increase the number of those that are called Turks."[243]

Clearly, the lineage of the Turkish people is mainly from the Armenians and Greeks of Mediterranean Europe, and less and less from the Turkic bloodline which was also

---

[242] Ghazarian, *Armenians in the Ottoman Empire*, xxiv; 91-92.

[243] Ghazarian, *Armenians in the Ottoman Empire*, 92.

an intermix of white people and non-white people from the beginning back on the Eastern Asian steppes. Therefore, "Turk" was no longer the racial or ethnic identity of these ruling Turkic Ghuzz; instead, it had developed into a symbol of political identity, and ultimately evolved into nothing more than a symbol of national identity.

Furthermore, in *The Cambridge History of Turkey*, history professor Ahmet Yasar Ocak of Turkey's Hacettepe University, gives an important narrative of the origins of the ethnic identity of the Turkish people from the perspective of a prominent scholar from Turkey. According to him, before the arrival of the Turks, the number and identity of the natives of the Anatolian plateau is unknown. Note that Ocak does not say they were Seljuk Turkic Ghuzz; rather he says they were "Oguz, also called Turkoman", and that this population had been "driven from Iran by the Great Seljuk rules."[244] Then, "at the time of the Turk's arrival the people of the region, called Rum in the Muslim sources, were composed of the original local population which had intermixed with the Greek population of the towns of western Anatolia and had become Christian."[245] In the eastern part of the plateau were mainly Georgian Armenians and Jacobite Christians

---

[244] Ahmet Yaşar Ocak, "Social, cultural and intellectual life, 1071-1453", in Kate Fleet (ed.), *The Cambridge History of Turkey, Volume I, Byzantium to Turkey, 1071-1453* (Cambridge University Press: UK, 2009), 361-362.

[245] Yaşar Ocak, "Social, cultural and intellectual life", 361.

(that is, Christians of the West-Syriac Church); while in the Mardin area of the south part of the plateau were "Suriyanis, Syriac-speaking Christians".[246] In addition, there were also Kurds who had long ago accepted Islam while under Arab conquest in the eastern and southwestern parts of the plateau, the region "which was known as Kurdistan", "and a section of them were Yazidi".[247]

The Turks "had only recently become Muslim"[248] following their migration to Anatolia. After the Battle of Manzikert, they "flowed en masse into Anatolia and began to settle" in the Anatolian plateau, and after a period of time, regarded this place as their new "homeland".[249] When the Mongols invaded Western Asia, many Turks also fled to Anatolia.[250] The Muslim Turks from both waves of migration mixed with the local Christian people, "particularly with the practice of taking girls from the Christian population"[251] and converting them to Islam. After the Mongols invaded, they also settled down in these beautiful grasslands from the 13th to the 15th centuries, converting to Islam in the 13th century. These Mongols were called Kara Tatars, and they intermixed with the

---

[246] Yaşar Ocak, "Social, cultural and intellectual life", 361.

[247] Yaşar Ocak, "Social, cultural and intellectual life", 361.

[248] Yaşar Ocak, "Social, cultural and intellectual life", 361-362.

[249] Yaşar Ocak, "Social, cultural and intellectual life", 362-363.

[250] Yaşar Ocak, "Social, cultural and intellectual life", 363.

[251] Yaşar Ocak, "Social, cultural and intellectual life", 364.

Turks, living in this area right up to the 1402 military invasion by the (Persianate Turko-Mongol) Timurid Empire.[252]

Ahmet Yasar Ocak also mentions that, according to different sources, although the vast majority of the Turkic Seljuk-Ghuzzs who settled in the Anatolia plateau already were Muslim, some were "Christian Turks who had converted to Nestorianism while still in Central Asia".[253] In the time of the Ottoman Empire, there still remained among the Ghuzz Turkish people some Christians who very likely believed in the same version of Christianity that their ancestors brought over from Central Asia, as well as some who had converted to the Greek Orthodox faith after moving there.[254] This is a very interesting point, because according to the research of a scholar, before the Turkic Ghuzz people of the Sogdia and Ili River valley-Tianshan mountains region left the area and headed west, they were a tribe of East-Syriac Christians; a son of their leader Seljuk, was a Christian.[255] This is further discussed in a later chapter.

From the above exploration, one may not find it hard to see that the ancestors of the people of Turkey were

---

[252] Yaşar Ocak, "Social, cultural and intellectual life", 365.

[253] Yaşar Ocak, "Social, cultural and intellectual life", 364.

[254] Yaşar Ocak, "Social, cultural and intellectual life", 364.

[255] Gao, *Ethnic Religions*, 280-281.

significantly mutated Turks from central Asia and not at all Uyghurs, though they possibly mingled with a very small number of Turkified Uyghurs from Kara-Khannid Khanate.

2. Clarifying the ethnic attributes in the historical names for the Hunnic-Turkic speaking people of Central Asia: *Oghuz, Ghuzz, Toquz Oghuz* and *Toquz Uyghur*

Various traces of confusion over the ethnic names of the Oghuz and Ghuzz can be found in the narratives about them in Arabic, Persian, Turkic, Turkish and even Uyghur historical texts. This has resulted in more complications in the discussion here of the origin of Turkey and Turkomen and how they are related to the Uyghurs. Ahmet Yasar Ocak says: "Turning to the Turks, the movement to and settlement in Anatolia of the Oğuz, also called Turkoman, who were the ancestors of the Turks of modern Turkey and had only become Muslim, began after the battle of Manzikert (Malazgirt)."[256] Then in the next paragraph he says that the Byzantines "were already familiar with the Guz (Oğuz) Turks who served in the Byzantine armies…"[257] Ocak's primary view appears to be that the Oghuz were the representative ancestors of the Turkish

---

[256] Ocak, "Social, cultural and intellectual life', 1071-1453", 361-362.

[257] Ocak, "Social, cultural and intellectual life'" 362.

people and the Turkoman, although he has a hard time with not placing "Guz" in this picture. Rene Grousset's approach is more cautious; he simply says that the forefathers of the Turkoman were either "Oghuz or Ghuz" without saying with certainty which one it was.[258]

Ocak's narrative seems to be derived from Muslim historical materials. In the *Compendium of the Languages of the Turks* completed in 1070s in Arabic by Mahmud Kashgari from Kashgar, this Uyghur scholar said, in the Kara-Khanid Khanate, "Oquz is Turkoman".[259] The question is then, who were the Oquz (also spelled Oghuz or Oğuz)? Rashiduddin Fazlullah obviously consulted the *Compendium of the Languages of the Turks* when writing his *Compendium of Chronicles*, completed in 1310-1311, but it goes a step further in providing a far more detailed narrative that clearly explains that Oghuz and his followers, who followed a monotheist faith, were the founding fathers of the Uyghur nation.[260] He also stated (inaccurately) that Turkomen were the mutated descendants of the Oghuz.[261] This Persian writer initially carefully avoids confusing the Turks with the Oghuz

---

[258] Grousset, *Empire*, 148.

[259] Kashagri, *Languages of the Turks* (vol. I), 62.

[260] Thackston, *Compendium of Chronicles*, 74-75.

[261] Thackston, *Compendium of Chronicles*, 31.

(Uyghur),[262] but then can't help but say, "Inasmuch as the Uyghurs are also Turks, and their habitation is near the realm of the Mongols,..."[263] The geographic location here indicates that it is indeed the Uyghurs who are being spoken of, and from the proof presented in my previous section we know that the Uyghurs and the Turks are not at all one and the same, and were even centuries-long enemies. Just as a Russian scholar pointed out, Rashiduddin, like most of his contemporaries, sometimes collectively called all of Asia's nomadic herding ethnic groups Turks and on occasion Mongols. That was the customary everyday usage at the time and not the terminology used in ethnography.[264] Be that as it may, the above-mentioned two works were, at the very least, saying that the Oghuz were Uyghurs and that the Turkoman were also Oghuz (this is not accurate).

The Persian geography book *The Regions of the World*, completed around 982, says in its "Discourse on the Toghuzghuz Country and its Towns" chapter, "East of it is the country of China; south of it, some parts of Tibet

---

[262] Thackston, *Compendium of Chronicles*, 30-31. On page 30 it says "This group was constantly with Oghuz". And "All the Uyghur tribes are descended from this group".

[263] Thackston, *Compendium of Chronicles*, 35.

[264] I. P. Petrushevsky, "Rashiduddin and His Works on the History" in Yu Dajun and Zhou Jianqi (tr.), *Rashiduddin Fazlullah's Compendium of Chronicles*, Chinese translation from Russian version (Beijing: The Commercial Press, 1983), 33-80, citing 66.

and the Khalukh; west of it, some parts of the Khirkhīz; north of it, also the Khirkhīz (who?) extend along all the Toghuzghuz country."[265] This is a fairly accurate description of the geographical location of the Kocho-Uyghur Khanate. However, according to the Turkic inscriptions on the ancient steles found on the Mongolian grasslands and Chinese historical materials, the name that should be used here is "Toghuz Oghuz", not Toghuz Ghuzz (or Toghuzghuz). In the chapter "Discourse on the Ghuz Country", the Persian author says: "East of this country is the Ghuz desert and the towns of Transoxiana; south of it, some parts of the same desert as well as the Khazar sea; west and north of it, the river Ātil."[266] Furthermore, the author, while making no comment about the Toghuz Oghuz, has this very negative description of the Ghuzz: "The Ghūz have arrogant faces (*shūkh-rūy*) and are quarrelsome (*sitīza-kār*), malicious (*badh-rag*), and malevolent (*hasud*)."[267] This seems to be an indirect way of saying that these Ghuzz people, despite having lived in Central Asia for a long time, still lagged far behind the Uyghurs in terms of level of civilization. Once again, the fairly accurate geographic description shows

---

[265] Vladimir Minorsky (tr. from Arabic and annotated), English version translated from Russian by Vasily Vladimirovich Barthold (or W. Barthold) with Preface, *The Regions of the World: A Persian Geography (Ḥudūd al-'Ālam), 372 A. H. --- 982 A.D* (London: University Press, Oxford, 1937), 94.

[266] Minorsky, *The Regions of the World*, 100.

[267] Minorsky, *The Regions of the World*, 100.

that the Ghuzz country was part of Turkoman. If then Toghuzghuz here is a misnomer and is obviously a reference to the Uyghurs, who then were the Toghuz Oghuz?

From this we can see that Muslim historical materials and Muslim academics are quite vague in their use of Oghuz and Ghuzz. Because of the great difficulty and even impossibility of finding non-Muslim written historical narratives in territories that were under Muslim rule for so long, the only option is to consult Muslim sources.[268] The inscriptions on those ancient steles erected by the Turks and Uyghurs refer variously to the *Toquz* Oghuzs, the *Sakiz* Oghuzs, the Oghuzs, the *On* Uyghurs, and the Uyghurs, but never mention the Ghuzzs. Furthermore, the earliest and the most detailed Chinese-language historical records about the Turks and the Uyghurs mentions the "Uyghurs" (using two different names in Chinese: *hui-he* and *hui-gu*), the "Nine Surnames Uyghurs", and the "Nine Surnames", but does not mention the Oghuzs or the Ghuzzs. Therefore, who the Oghuzs, the *Toquz* Oghuzs, the Ghuzzs, and the Uyghurs were is a difficult question that academia has been pondering and arguing over[269] for the past century.

For instance, the French scholar of Turkic studies J. Hamilton reads "Toquz Oghuz" as a version of the ancient

---

[268] Richards, *The Annals of the Saljuq Turks*, 8.

[269] Minorsky, *The Regions of the World: A Persian Geography*, 266.

Turkic language term "toquz oghush" that means "nine surnames". His is a widely accepted view,[270] and it would be hard to take exception with this hypothesis if only the Turkic language inscriptions on the Turkic and Uyghur steles are more carefully examined. In addition, if Chinese-language historical materials are consulted and then compared with the Turkic language inscriptions and Muslim materials, then it is clear that this hypothesis is not sound; that's because in these texts, "Toquz Oghuz" means "nine surnames Oghuz", which in turn means "nine surnames Uyghur" in the Chinese texts. Otherwise, how does one explain "Toquz Tatar" or "Uch (three) Karluks" in the Uyghur Moyan Chor Inscription?

Clarifying the above names will have a direct bearing on the correct understanding of the ethnic and historical records in the identity of modern Turkey's people, modern Turks (Turkoman) and modern Uyghurs. Below is a comprehensive look at the Turkic language and Chinese-language inscriptions on these Turkic and Uyghur steles, as well as Chinese-language historical records from Tang China.

First, according to the Turkic language version of those ancient Turkic and Uyghur steles, that is, the first-hand materials of the Turks and the Uyghurs about their own names, the rendering of the Uyghur related ethnic

---

[270] Geng, *Turkic Inscriptions,* 138-139.

name in Latin letters is "Toquz Oɣuz".[271] Based on the pronunciation of contemporary Uyghur, this can be written as "Toqquz Oğuz", which in turn can be written in English as "Tokhuz Oghuz". The steles dating from the Turk's khanates—for example, the Tonyuquq Inscription (716-725)—refer to the "Oɣuz" and "Toquz Oɣuz" as enemies of the Turks.[272] "Uyɣur" and "Oɣuz" both appear on the Bilga Khan Inscription (734),[273] where the first use of the Uyghur (Uyɣur) name appears. This is just before the Uyghurs overthrew the Turk's khanate and established their Uyghur khanate. Note that both these commemorative steles were erected by the Turks. Of the commemorative steles erected by the Uyghur Khanate, on the north side of the Moyan Chor Khan Inscription, erected in approximately 759 in praise of the Uyghur Khanate's second khan, "*on* uyɣur toquz oɣuz" shows up in the same sentence and is translated as "*On* Uyghurs and Toquz Oghuz".[274] This, then, shows that there is a difference between "Uyghur" and Oghuz", which makes the whole matter even more complicated.

Second, Chinese-language historical records offer detailed and reliable information that can help further

---

[271] See the 9th line in the Turkic text on the south face of the Tonyuquq Inscription. Geng, *Turkic Inscriptions*, 96.

[272] Geng, *Turkic Inscriptions*, 96.

[273] Geng, *Turkic Inscriptions*, 163.

[274] Geng, *Turkic Inscriptions*, 194.

clarify the meanings of these names. The *NBoT* says that when the Uyghurs established their kingdom, they occupied all of the territory known as "the Land of the Nine Surnames", that is, the northern part of the Mongolian grasslands, and lists in detail these "nine surnames," the first being Yaghlaqar (Yaɣlaqar), which the text states "is a Uyghur surname".[275] The *NBoT* also says "the Karluks and the Nine Surnames [Oghuz] established the Uyghur *yabghu*, known as the *Huai-ren* khan."[276] According to brief research conducted by the great Chinese sinologist Wang Guowei on the Chinese-language version of the text on the famous Karabalgasun stele, the *OBoT* says that in the third year of the *Yuan-he* reign of Emperor Xian-zong (808), "On the *Bing-wu* day [in May], the emperor conferred on the Nine Surname Uyghur Khan the title of 'Tangrida qut bolmish alp bilga Bao-yi Khan'".[277] This may be the only mention in ancient Chinese-language historical records of the "Nine Surnames Uyghurs," even though the Uyghurs are repeatedly referred to while mention is never made of "Oghuz" or "Ghuzz." Also, of the three languages that

---

[275] Ou-yang, *NBoT*, "Uyghurs I", 4651. "悉有九姓地"。

[276] Ou-yang, *NBo.*, "Uyghurs II", 4670. "葛禄与九姓复立回纥叶护，所谓怀仁可汗者也。"

[277] Liu, *OBoT,* No. 14 *Ben-ji*, *Xian-zong I,* 288; Wang, *Guantang Jilin*, vol. 20, f19r: "Comment on Nine Surname Uyghur Khan Stele". 五月"丙午，正衙册九姓回纥可汗为登啰里汨蜜施合毗伽保义可汗。"（王国维：《观堂集林》）

appear on the Karabalgasun stele, the Chinese text is the best-preserved, while most of the Turkic text has been lost and the Sogdian text is somewhat better preserved than the Turkic. More important is the Chinese title of the stele engraved at the top of the stele: "Inscription accompanied by preface [in praise] of Ay Tängridä Qut Bulmïš Alp Bilgä Qaghan of the Uighurs consisting of nine tribes for his sacred scholarship and divine martial virtue";[278] in Chinese, shortened to simply "Nine Surnames Uyghur Khan Stele".

Third, the full Chinese name of the inscription is sufficient to prove that "Nine Surnames Uyghurs" is the Chinese translation for "Toquz Oghuz". At the same time, by comparing the inscription with what's recorded in the *OBoT*, it is clear that this is the same khan to whom Tang-China conferred the title of khan. In the *OBoT*, the Chinese characters for the title "*Bao-yi* Khan" that was conferred on him are added after his Uyghur title, while the Chinese text on the Karabalgasun stele bears only his full Uyghur title. Furthermore, the Sogdian version of the name of this inscription has only one more word than the Chinese name, while a few more words appear in the Turkic language version of the khan's title; the basic meaning remains the same. Most importantly, in all three languages, the term "stele of the Uyghur khan" rather than

---

[278] "KARABALGASUN ii. The Inscription", Encyclopaedia Iranica, accessed 26 July 2018,
http://www.iranicaonline.org/articles/karabalgasun-the-inscription.

"Oghuz khan" is used.[279] The same is true of contemporaneous Tang-China historical records, which without exception all use "Uyghur" as the official name and not "Oghuz". This means that "Uyghur" is the corresponding Chinese name of "Oghuz", even though the two terms are used separately in the Uyghurs' Turkic-language Moyan Chor inscription.

Thus, this careful comparison of the aforementioned Turkic and Uyghur inscriptions and Chinese-language historical records reveals that the latter uses only "Nine Surnames Uyghur" or "Uyghur" for Toquz Oghuz, Oghuz and Uyghur. That is to say, the authors of the Tang-China histories regarded them as one and the same. It also shows that "Toquz" is "nine surnames," and that "Uyghur" was but one of these surnames (tribes) while the Uyghur leader was the first khan of the Uyghur khanate. In other words, Nine Surnames is the shortest abbreviation for the confederation of these nine tribes, of which the Uyghurs, whose surname was Yaghlaqar, was one. That's why many Uyghur khans were later all surnamed Yaghlaqar. In this way, when the Uyghur leader *Yaghbu* became khan, "Uyghur" became the representative name for this alliance, and this nine-tribe confederation became the Uyghur kingdom, with the Uyghur tribe forming the nucleus of the leadership. Consequently, this khanate can also be called the "Nine Surname Uyghurs". Hence, the

---

[279] Lin and Gao, *Uyghur History*, 396, 398, 403.

tribal name of "Uyghur" became the name for the khanate and the confederation. Therefore, it becomes easy to understand why the Moyan Chor Inscription also refers to "*on* Uyghur toquz Oghuz" together: the first part ("*on* Uyghur" or Ten Surnames Uyghur) is the name for the confederation and the khanate consisting of ten tribes while the latter part ("toquz Oghuz" or Nine Surnames Oghuz) is the appellation for the ethnic group consisting of nine tribes, while Oghuz is the name of their ethnicity. The *NBoT* also says that the Uyghurs also united with their allies the Basmyls and the Karluks "for a total of 11 surnames, each under one ruler, and called 11 tribes".[280] Thus, two more allies were added to the newly established kingdom, totaling 11 surname-tribes, that is, the Eleven Surnames Uyghurs.

In summary, the Oghuz and *Toquz* Oghuz mentioned in the Turkic language inscriptions on the Turkic and Uyghur steles were one and the same, with the former referring to the Oghuz people and the latter referring to the confederation of nine Oghuz tribes. That's why the inscriptions frequently used "the Oghuz people" and "Toquz Oghuz people" interchangeably. Among the *Toquz* Oghuz were Uyghurs surnamed "Yaghlaqar" or "royal tribe", which includes many Uyghur khans such as the founding father of the Orkhon Uyghur Empire; these Oghuz were those called "Uyghurs" in the Turkic

---

[280] Ou-yang, *NBoT*, "Uyghurs I", 4651. "总十一姓，并置都督，号十一部落"。

language inscriptions because *NBoT* says "the surname of Uyghur is Yaghlaqar" and "Yaghlaqar is surname of Uyghur".[281] After the Uyghur Khanate was founded, or re-established, the Toquz Oghuz could also be called the Toquz Uyghurs; the former still referring to the name of the people of the confederation of tribes, the latter to the united khanate. As for the reference to the "On Uyghurs and Toquz Oghuzs" on the Moyan Chor stele, it refers to the *On* Uyghur Khanate made up of the Uyghurish Karluks and the nucleus of the "nine surnames Oghuz tribes" and means, "the Uyghur United Khanate and the Confederation of the Nine Surnames Oghuz Tribes". The former is the Uyghur United Khanate, consisting of ten tribes; the latter is the original confederation of which the Uyghurs were a part. These concepts reflected by these names are indeed easily confused, just as with the terms "China", "Chinese people", and "Han people" in Chinese texts. Note that the Karluks split off and left the Uyghur confederation sometime after 758, which means that the Moyan Chor stele was erected some time before the split.

Therefore, both the *Compendium of the Languages of the Turks* and *Compendium of Chronicles* are inaccurate in placing the Oghuz as the direct ancestors of the Turkmens. But the *Compendium of the Languages of the Turks* is quite accurate in its explanation of where the

---

[281] Ou-yang, *NBoT*, "Uyghurs I", 4649, "回纥姓药罗葛氏";4651, "药罗葛，回纥姓也"。

"Uyghur" people were located in relation to the locations of the other Turkic speaking tribes, including the "Oghuz", as well as the locations of the Khitans and the Chinese.[282] That is, this Uyghur Muslim linguistic scholar separated "Oghuz" from "Uyghur", and sidesteps the issue of the Toquz. Furthermore, he later says that "Uyghur" is also the name of a nation with five cities called Sulmi, Kocho, Chanbalik, Beshbalik and Yangibali;[283] this shows that it is none other than the Kocho-Uyghur kingdom. An earlier Persian Islamic historical text, *The Regions of the World* differentiates the *Toquz* Oghuz and the Ghuzz, and describes the location of the Ghuzz kingdom, which is precisely the kingdom of the later Turkmen (Turkoman) people. Therefore, combining the information from these two sources, it's possible to confirm that the Turkmen are not the descendants of the Uyghurs, nor were they the descendants of the Toquz Oghuz; rather they were the descendants of the Ghuzz.[284] So the "Oghuz" mentioned in the *Compendium of the Languages of the Turks* as the forefathers of the Turkmen correspond to the "Ghuzz" forefathers of the Turkmen in *The Regions of the World*.

The origin of the name Turkmen is itself quite complicated. Its first appearance was in the late 8th century in Tang-China historical records (which suggests

---

[282] Kashagri, *Languages of the Turks* (vol. 1), 31.

[283] Kashagri, *Languages of the Turks* (vol. 1), 120, 122.

[284] Gao, *Ethnic Religions*, 280.

that the Turkmen were related to the Western Turks); it began to appear in Muslim historical records in the latter half of the 10th century. [285] There are two basic explanations for the meaning of this name: 1) "resembling a Turk"; or 2) "Islam-believing Turks".[286] According to my research mentioned earlier, originally their ancestors, the Turks, were the white *Hu* intermixed with non-white people of East Asia; intermixing became easier after they moved to central Asia where the natives were white Indo-Europeans and became the dominant ruling group, so I am inclined to the first explanation as the original meaning,[287] even though the second one became legitimate in at least the time of the Mongol Empire. To summarize, the Ghuzz, the forefathers of the Turkmen, were the descendants of the Ten Surnames (or Ten Arrows) Tribes of the Western Turks[288] further intermixed with local Indo-Europeans, not the descendants of the *Toquz* Oghuz (Uyghurs), while the forefathers of the Turkish people were, as mentioned

---

[285] Li Shuhui, "Studies on Tyrkmen", *The Silk Road* (Lanzhou, Northwest Normal University: No. 12 issue of 2017, total 349 issues), 5-10, citing 5.（李树辉:《突厥蛮研究》）

[286] Li Shuhui, "Studies on Tyrkmen", 5-6.

[287] In 751, Arab forces defeated the Chinese army, becoming the masters of Central Asia, and ruling over the native Indo-Europeans, who were in the majority, and the Turks. Since the earliest use of the term Turkmen occurs in late-8th century Tang-China historical records, this means it is unlikely they were Muslim Turks, because it's unlikely that the Turks would have converted so quickly and in such great numbers to the faith of their conquerors.

[288] Liu, *Old Book of Tang*, "Turks I", 3526.

earlier, simply the Seljuk Turks, who were another branch of the Ghuzz people. It's important to note that in the famous Muslim historical text *The Perfect or The Complete [Work] of History*, its author Ibn al-Athir (who died in 1233) refers to the Seljuk Turks also as the Oghuz Turks.[289] This is also not accurate, although the convenience that the usage of this simplified generic shorthand brings to the narrative is quite understandable.

Finally, in terms of their ethnic attributes, including physical traits and language, today's Turkish people and Turkmen are close to each other, both being descendants of the Western Turks, or "ten arrows" Turks, whose bloodlines had mixed to a very high degree with the native Indo-Europeans. Today's Uyghurs and Uzbeks are also close, both being descendants of the Kocho-Uyghurs and the Kara-Khanid Uyghurs, but in comparison with the Turkish people and the Turkmen, their bloodlines are mixed to a much lesser degree with the native white Indo-Europeans.

3. The pre-1949 struggles of the Uyghur people on identity restoration

According to research by the American Uyghur scholar Justin Jon Rudelson, it was the 'symbolic image of the

---

[289] Richards, *The Annals of the Saljuq Turks*, 2, 13.

non-Islamic and thus "pure"' and the "highly developed" Uyghur Khanate before their Turpan Uyghur culture (what I call the Kocho civilization) had contact with Islam and the Persian culture that profoundly influenced Turkey's founder Mustafa Kemal Ataturk (1881—1938) to re-orient the modern Turkish people's ethnic "purity" and national identity.[290] Hence, we see in the 1922-1923 process of guiding the establishment of the Republic of Turkey that Ataturk—through abolishing the Islamic sultanate and imams systems, expelling members of the Ottoman royal family, disbanding Islamic courts and schools, banning women's veils and other Islamic apparel, ending the use of the Islamic code of law, adopting the Latin script to replace the Arabic and Persian scripts in the Turkish language, etc.—used a series of secularizing radical reforms to put into practice this new ideal of a "de-Islamified" Turkish state and ethnic identity, and became an autocratic first president of Turkey. The fact that he also de-emphasized what is called "pan-Turkism", "instead encouraging Turkish nationalism within Turkey",[291] should not be overlooked.

Furthermore, the late 19th century Turkic speaking Jadidist Tatar educational reform movement that began in Russia and was suppressed by the Soviet Union

---

[290] Rudelson, *Oasis Identities*, 31.

[291] "Pan-Turkism, POLITICAL MOVEMENT, TURKEY", Encyclopedia Britannica, accessed 26 July 2018, https://www.britannica.com/topic/Pan-Turkism.

Communist government gradually evolved into a new social reform movement, and without doubt provided experience and motivation to Turkey's socio-political revolution. From its inception, the Jadidist movement opposed the shackles of conservative forces in Islam through new model Western-style education and publications. In 1900 in Ghulja (Ili, or Yining, Xinjiang), an existing school was re-opened as a Jadidist New Method school operated by Husayn Musabayev, who was from a successful Artush business family, with support from local Qing China government officials. In 1904, a teacher who had been sent in 1902 to study at the Imperial School of Civil Administration in Istanbul returned and became the head of the school.[292] In 1912, after appeasing the influential local anti-Jadidist figure Akhunbayevs, Adbulqadir Damolla opened Kashgar's first New Method school. A primary school with a Jadidist program, though, was opened as early 1885 by Husayn Musabayev in Artush.[293]

The new cultural movement which spread quickly throughout Xinjiang could not ultimately avoid evolving into a movement for the restoration of ethnic identity and from that into a revolutionary political agenda. The Jadidist movement was similar to China's New Youth movement of the early 20th century; both came about

---

[292] Brophy, *Uyghur Nation*, 95-96.
[293] Brophy, *Uyghur Nation*, 112; Millward, *Crossroads*, 172.

because of the reflections and castigation provoked by the strong force of Western civilization; both were committed to cultural and social transformation against tradition, and both were striving for modernization and progress for the nation. Nevertheless, the influence of Islam, the religious attribute of the Uyghur identity, on Xinjiang's Jadidist movement and the process of restoring the Uyghur identity cannot be overlooked. For instance, the passionate sponsor of the New Method School, Husayn Musabayev, went to Mecca for his *Hajj* in 1907.[294]

In 1913, Husayn Musabayev sent a delegation to Istanbul, "to request a modern-educated teacher from Mehmed Talat Pas, who was then in charge of an organisation promoting pan-Turkism and pan-Islam outside Turkey", and the latter sent the teacher Ahmed Kemal.[295] He and six other teachers arrived in Kashgar on March 14, 1914;[296] the six others ended up teaching in other cities in Xinjiang.[297] Teaching in the Artush Normal School, "Ahmed Kemal used textbooks produced in Istanbul. ...and the students were told the Ottoman sultan was their supreme ruler."[298] The letters and books written from the 1910s through the 1920s by the then Xinjiang

---

[294] Brophy, *Uyghur Nation*, 104.

[295] Millward, *Crossroads*, 172.

[296] Date and number of the group refers to Li, *Xinjiang*, 169.

[297] Millward, *Crossroads*, 173.

[298] Millward, *Crossroads*, 173.

governor Yang Zengxin showed that he was very alert to the steadily growing influence of Ottoman Istanbul's religious-political ideology in the Xinjiang region.[299] He was vigilant especially with respect to "Great Hui Religion in Unity"[300] (pan-Islam) and adopted a series of boycott measures, including expelling Ottoman Turkish teachers, closing down schools, and strict inspection of mail and published materials sent from Ottoman Turkey. In 1917, he banned Xinjiang Muslims from going on pilgrimage to Mecca, a ban that lasted for 10 years.[301] As early as 1879, the British ambassador to China told Qing dynasty officials that the Ottoman court had secretly dispatched envoys to Kashgar.[302]

In Turkey in the 1920s, critics accused Ataturk of betraying Islam, pursuing secularization, and being blindly Westernized. In fact, looking at Ataturk's insistence on the Asian political tradition of a ruling one-party system and rejection of Western-style democracy, his methods were not Westernization but rather an effort to revive the Turkish people's pure, pre-Islam ethnic identity. That is why he stressed the importance of the Turkic history of the Turkish people and their earlier history on the Anatolian

---

[299] Li, *Xinjiang*, 170-71.

[300] *Da Yi Hui Jiao Zhu Yi* means "promoting the unifying Great *Hui* religion", i.e. Islam.

[301] Li, *Xinjiang*, 171-172.

[302] Brophy, *Uyghur Nation*, 90.

plateau. In addition, Ataturk in 1930s "ordered linguists to purge the Turkish language of Arabic and Persian elements."[303] The background of Ataturk pursuing in this way was largely due to the Turkological discoveries from the long-lost Turkic past and the Uyghur historical legacy by the Russian and other western scholars at the turn of the century producing "Uyghurism" which represents a long lost pride of the forgotten Turkic past including one version on "a Uyghur historic golden age as part of the heritage of all Turkic-speaking peoples."[304] The lost glorification of the Uyghurs became "an internal part of late-Ottoman Turkism and Turanism" and the advocacy held that "Uyghurs who lived in cities were naturally more advanced" than "the primitive and nomadic Turks" who were shepherds".[305] Here most importantly, such a view is in regards Ottoman Turkish people, with Hungarians and Finns as among the most advanced Uyghurs.[306] So at that time the Turkish elites wanted to be part of the Uyghurs, not vice versa as we see today.

Therefore 'In Atatürk's new Pure Turkish lexicon (*öz Türkçe*), the name "Uyghur" was adopted as the word *uyğar*, substituting for the Arabic *madani*, meaning "civilized"'.[307] Clearly, the brilliant civilization that was

---

[303] Brophy, *Uyghur Nation*, 143.
[304] Brophy, *Uyghur Nation*, 142-143.
[305] Brophy, *Uyghur Nation*, 142-143.
[306] Brophy, *Uyghur Nation*, 142.
[307] Brophy, *Uyghur Nation,*, 143.

created by the "pure", original identity of the Kocho-Uyghurs before they became Islamified gave this far-sighted, sagacious "father" of Turkey unwavering confidence and motivation by example,[308] not to mention the abundant resources of the brilliant Western civilization that were close at hand which could be directly picked up and utilized.

Over the course of the previous 1200 years of Asian history, the influence that the Uyghur civilization that originated on the Mongolian steppes, especially the later Kocho (Turpan) Uyghur civilization of Xinjiang, had on other ethnic kingdoms to the east, including that of the Mongols, as well as China, all the way to west Asia cannot be ignored. At the same time, from Tang-China to the Mongol Empire, the Uyghurs were also influenced by the Han-Chinese, Turks, Sogdian and Tocharian civilizations we well as by Manichaeism and Christianity. For instance, in addition to the writings of Manichaeism, Christianity and Buddhism, the archeological finds in Turpan have included books written in Uyghur on research of Chinese *I Ching* and its divinations, as well as translations in Uyghur of the Greek "Aesop's Fables".[309] Evidence of the Han-Chinese influence on the Uyghurs can be seen in the famous tri-lingual Karabalgasun inscription, which is

---

[308] Rudelson, *Oasis Identities,* 31.

[309] Tōru Haneda, *Survey to the History of Western Regions' Civilizations* (tr. Zheng Yuanfang; Shanghai: Commercial Press, 1934), 78, 80. 羽田亨（日）著，郑元方译：《西域文明史概论》

written in Turkic, Sogdian, and Han-Chinese. Also, the *Compendium of the Languages of the Turks* mentions that the Kocho Uyghurs not only used the Turkic script with its 24 letters, that is the Uyghur script, but also that official letters and documents used script similar to that used by the Qin people.[310] Because the *Compendium* also states that the Tabghach were the Qin people[311] and because all the steles erected by the Turks and Uyghurs refer to the Chinese as Tabghach,[312] this was clearly a reference to Han-Chinese.

The Uyghur poet Abdukhaliq, who was famous in Xinjiang in the 1920s and 1930s, is but one example of someone who was influenced by the Jadidist movement and was possessed of a similar mindset, ideas and insights, and was committed to restoring the Uyghur identity that existed before it was subjugated by Islam. In the same way, Deng Xiaoping's reform movement in China in the 1980s using the slogan of economic construction was in fact a further step toward "redefining" ethnic and national identity through "de-Communization" by following Engel's Communist Second International, that is, the Soviet Khrushchev revisionist road.

---

[310] Kashgari, *Languages of Turks*, 32, 479.

[311] Kashgari, *Languages of Turks*, 479.

[312] Geng, *Turkic Inscriptions*, 94, 96, 203, 222.

In conclusion, the sense of identity between the Uyghurs and the Turkish people seriously lacks an adequate intersection of ethnic, geographic or historical attributes while emphasizing the pan-Islam religious attribute and pan-Turkic political symbols. Indeed, this can only result in weakening or even marginalizing the unique Uyghur identity. This has the same effect as when Islamic forces historically renamed the Uyghurs "Turks". It was precisely this kind of a generic Turkic symbol which assimilated Uyghur unique identity, that Abdukhaliq and his *Jadidist* comrades tried hard to cast off and were quite successful in doing so, though unfortunately only for a short period. The efforts today in Xinjiang and worldwide to find ways to revise and reemphasize the Uyghur ethnic attribute into a Turkish and Turkic one is the manifestation of the desire of political and religious forces to confuse the reconstruction of the Uyghur identity.

Historically, Islam was the most effective in changing the ethnic identity of the Uyghur people, as well as of the Ghuzz Turks, because through this religious belief, not only the Uyghur written language changed, but even the name of the ethnic group changed. Beginning in 1450, that is at the height of the Mongol Chagatai Khanate's forcing of Islam on Xinjiang, the use of the term Uyghur was ended for nearly 500 years.[313] It appears to have been mainly due to the influence of the famous Uyghur poet

---

[313] Rudelson, *Oasis Identities*, 5.

Abdukhaliq, who adopted "Uyghur" as his pen name,[314] and the impetus given by the Soviet consul-general in Urumqi, Garegin Apresoff, as well as the crucial initiative of Burhan Shahidi, who was a Tatar friend of the Uyghur poet and would later become the first governor of the Xinjiang Communist government, that the Xinjiang Sheng Shicai Chinese government in 1934 officially decided to resume use of the name Uyghur.[315]

The ruler of the quasi-independent Xinjiang government, Sheng Shicai, a ruthless Han Chinese governor possibly of Manchurian blood who was responsible for the execution of Abdukhaliq in 1933(one year before the ethnonym "Uyghur" was restored), adopted the liberal policy of Communist Soviet "to recognize fourteen ethnic categories in Xinjiang" with "Uyghur" listed as number one and "Taranchi" as number two (the Taranchi were Uyghurs from the Zhetysu region including Ili).[316] Not surprisingly, the famous Uyghur intellectual Muhammad Emin Bughrato criticized Sheng's categories, insisting that "Turk" or "Turki" was sufficient designation for the Turkic speaking Muslims in Xinjiang because of the "political implications [that were] threatening to divide Muslim and Turkic peoples against

---

[314] Rudelson, *Oasis Identities*, 149; Ding and Zhang, *Chinese Muslims*, 204-205.

[315] Rudelson, *Oasis Identities*, 149.

[316] Millward, *Crossroads*, 208.

each other".[317] Interestingly Uzbek was listed as a different category from Uyghur even though both are descended from the ancient Uyghurs and speak nearly identical languages.

It is not a surprise that even today some scholars writing in English are still following this track by using "Turki" [Turk] as the name of Uyghurs with a certain excuse,[318] or in a better gesture by placing Uyghurs under the broader Turkic ethnicity.[319] "The rhetoric of Turkic or Muslim unity, I suggest," as David Brophy whose work clearly and neatly differentiates Uyghur from Turk and only as "Turkic-speaking" people[320] commented on the Uyghur identity issue in 1920s, "should be seen as primarily expressing a political position…and not a theoretical stance on the ideal boundaries of the nation."[321] Unfortunately, that is still true today with the addition of religious or ideological positions, even in academia.

In a similar way, the Chinese (Xinjiang) government defines Uyghurs as a group part of the *Zhong-hua* ethnic category which is pan-Chinese (*zhong hua min zu da jia*

---

[317] Millward, *Crossroads*, 208-209.

[318] Ildikó Bellér-Hann, *Community Matters in Xinjiang, 1880-1949 towards a Historical Anthropology of the Uyghur* (Leiden; Boston: Brill, 2008), 49, 51.

[319] Millward, *Crossroads*, 31.

[320] Brophy, *Uyghur Nation,* 1.

[321] Brophy, *Uyghur Nation,* 247.

ting) and clearly labels the narrative of "those ethnic groups in Xinjiang are not part of *Zhong hua* min zu" as anti-political correctness.[322] In fact, according to my research on Chinese classics from the Han and Tang dynasties, Uyghurs belonged to what Chinese historians and the dynastic governments referred to as the *Zhong-xia* ethnic category (*zhong xia min zu da jia ting*).[323] The combination of these two general categories is the *Hua-xia* ethnic category (*Hua xia min zu*) which has not been mentioned officially by the Chinese government and intellectuals any more in recent decades. Nevertheless, the victory from the rescue and restoration of the ethnonym "Uyghur" by those Uyghur intellectuals in the 1910s-1930s through the wave of "Uyghurism" still stands firm despite the challenges. Today I recommend that the

---

[322] "Correcting Views on the Historical Xinjiang Issues", People's Daily, accessed 28 October 2018,
http://paper.people.com.cn/rmrb/html/2018-10/28/nw.D110000renmrb_20181028_1-08.htm.(《正确认识新疆历史问题》,新疆维吾尔自治区中国特色社会主义理论体系研究中心,刊登于《人民日报》2018年10月28日第8版)

[323] 根据《汉书》匈奴传第64上,"然至冒顿,而匈奴最强大,尽服从北夷,而南与诸夏为敌国,……"这里说明了诸夏是在匈奴和中国之间,也就是那些白种狄人,匈奴还不属于夏。隋唐时期,中国将北方草原地区通称为中夏,或夏地。根据《隋书·突厥》可知,隋朝末年,突厥人势力壮大,"势凌中夏"。又根据《唐大诏令集》卷129的《(大中十一年)册回鹘可汗文》,唐宣宗鼓励西迁庞特勤回鹘回到长城以北的草原,重新复国,因为"华夏屏卫,理宜常存"。这里将中国称为"华",回鹘汗国称为"夏"。

Uyghur elites take a step further to fortify the victory by designating modern Uyghurs (and possibly Uzbeks) as the Tlughish and even Uyghurish speaking group instead of the Turkic speaking group.

Successful restoration of the original appellation "Uyghur" resulted largely, though not solely, from the contribution of Abdukhaliq who was fluent in Chinese (he adopted a Chinese name: Ha-wen-cai), as well as Russian (having studied in the Soviet Union for three years in the 1920s), and became a Jadidist.[324] He discovered, through reading and studying China's historical texts and later making the acquaintance of some Soviet Turkologists, the history of his own ethnic group and its related civilization.[325] Other factors leading to the restoration of "Uyghur" included the February 1918 founding of a club called "Uyghur" in Vernyi (Almaty) by Taranchi Uyghurs whose leader was Abdullah Rozibaqiev.[326] Another famous Uyghur intellectual was Nazarkhoja Abdusamadov, a Taranchi from Ghaljat who used the pen name "Uyghur's Child" as early as the 1910s.[327] Also, a Taranchi student named Abdulhayy Muhammadi studying in Tashkent published a poem called "My Young Heart" in the student journal *Young Uyghur* in 1922 that mentioned

---

[324] Brophy, *Uyghur Nation*, 246; Rudelson, *Oasis Identities*, 149.

[325] Rudelson, *Oasis Identities*, 148-149.

[326] Brophy, *Uyghur Nation*, 155-156.

[327] Brophy, *Uyghur Nation*, 139, 141.

"Uyghuristan"[328] in 1926, he published his *Principles of Uyghur Orthography* in Moscow.[329]

The whole movement of identity restoration started by Jadidism-influenced Uyghur intellectuals and elites from the Taranchi area and Turpan is in essence a turning away from a five century long identity-dissimilation after the Islamic conquest by the Eastern Chagatai Mongols and from the Ottoman-Turkish ideology of pan-Islam and pan-Turkism which runs counter to pan-Christianity and pan-Europeanism, as well as pan-Iranism and pan-Slavism. However, in Kashgar, the Islamic center of Xinjiang, Jadidist reform seemed devoid of any passion regarding the restoration of the use of "Uyghur", which is probably due to the Kashgar Uyghur's historical sense of identity as Islamic Kara-Khanids with a more mutated bloodline from intermixing with the Indo-European natives, like their kinsmen the Uzbeks, on the other side of Pamir mountains.

Although the Jadidist movement that began in the early 20th century in Xinjiang did not start out with the aim of seeking political independence for the Uyghur people,[330] the successful restoration of the ethnic name inevitably aroused memories related to the history of the Uyghur Khanate, from which came the need for a new

---

[328] Brophy, *Uyghur Nation,* 185.

[329] Brophy, *Uyghur Nation,* 226.

[330] Millward, *Crossroads,* 176.

sense of political identity. As a result, the "dual pan-" ideology and propaganda that began in Russia and was adopted and promoted by Ottoman Turkey[331] provided the direction and motivation for this practice, just like the political influence of Soviet Marxism-Leninism on China's New Culture Movement. In the 1930s and 1940s, the "Turkic Islamic Republic of East Turkestan" was established first in Kashgar and then in Ili; both were short-lived. In terms of the name of this state, originally the "Republic of Uyhuristan" but soon after changed, the development of the Jadidist Movement in Xinjiang was ultimately fettered by the "dual pan-" framework, whereas the founder of modern Turkey, Ataturk, was able to break out of this framework.

In their long history, the Uyghurs and their civilization were significantly changed by the Turkified-Islam-induced transformation of the ethnic and religious attributes of their identity and by Islam's enduring hold on the Uyghurs thereafter. However, the triumph of this monotheistic religion was actually not very thorough. It might be a surprise to some that the Shamanism that the Uyghur ancestors believed in is still alive and active in the lives of the Uyghurs today. According to the observations and research of one modern Uyghur anthropologist, "Among the Uyghur masses looking for shamans today

---

[331] "Pan-Turkism", Encyclopedia Britannica, accessed 27 July 2018, https://www.britannica.com/topic/Pan-Turkism.

are teachers at colleges and universities, government officials, students preparing for important exams, and ordinary citizens."[332] Because the Shaman culture is one that any monotheistic religion must reject and exclude, Shamanistic activities among the Uyghurs can only take place and survive by borrowing an Islamic "overcoat".[333] The aforementioned scholar cannot help but ask: Why has the Shaman culture been so enduring in the Uyghur culture, and why does it continue to be popular among the Uyghurs today and among other Turkic speaking Islamic ethnic groups? The scholar makes this profound point:

> In this rapidly changing, highly competitive modern society, people are desperately paying close attention to and want to know their future and their fate, or the direction of a specific event, or even the result of some private secret that cannot be revealed. The answers to these questions cannot be obtained from the Islamic clerics, so this sense of insecurity propels this group of believers towards shamans, or, put another way, people

---

[332] Reyihanguli Yimamu, "Multi-cultural Accumulation: the Hybridity of Uyghure Shamanism Belief", *Nationalities Research in Qinghai* (Xining, China: Qinghai Nationalities University, School of Ethnology and Sociology, vol. 24, no. 2 issue, 2013), 99-103, citing 99. （热依汗古丽•依玛木：《多元并蓄试论维吾尔族萨满信仰的"混杂状态"》，刊登于《青海民族研究》）

[333] Yimamu, "Multi-cultural Accumulation", 102.

expect the shamans in their lives to solve their problems and ease their anxieties for them.[334]

The fact that Shamanism continues to exist and remains popular today shows that Islam is not necessarily able to truly satisfy the needs of the religious attribute of the Uyghur identity and is more a religious-political ideological tool to control their ethnic identity. It is similar to the institutional Communist-Socialist belief used as an ideological-political tool to control the Chinese national identity. It therefore also shows that the religious attribute of the Uyghur identity is still an open question, and that from this perspective the millennium-long rule of Islam has not necessarily been a complete success. This kind of subconscious openness of the religious attribute without doubt aggravates the Uyghur identity crisis and makes the issue of the Uyghur identity's reconstruction even more urgent. At the same time, the insecurity created not only by modern society but also the Chinese Communist government's iron curtain reign have induced the Uyghurs to urgently and anxiously seek an identity reorientation. Therefore, the claim by some Uyghurs of "returning to Islam" is nothing more than an option where there are no other options. Meanwhile, Christianity, as a monotheistic religion, has also had the ability in the past three decades to influence some Uyghur elites and urban residents.

---

[334] Yimamu, "Multi-cultural Accumulation", 102

Post-colonialism theorist Homi K. Bhabha proposed (1994) the anthropological concept of "homelessness" among certain social groups that was later expanded upon by Harvard social anthropologist Michael D. Jackson (2000). According to this concept, some groups of people are forever in a dissociative, unsettled state of "hybridity".[335] The Uyghurs have been in a continuous state of this kind of dissociative "hybridity" since their 841 flight west from the Mongolian steppes, and especially after their Kocho civilization was exterminated by Mongol Islamic forces in the late 14th century. The identity crisis and the urgency to reconstruct an identity that have resulted from this state of hybridity due to nearly nine centuries of alternating rule by foreign ethnic groups with their foreign religions or ideologies, especially the rule of the past 70 years by the atheist Chinese Communist government with socialism, have reached a historic peak. Under these circumstances, pan-Islamism and pan-Turkism, with the Turkish national model, have become the spiritual, psychological, cultural and political capitals from which the Uyghur religious attribute and ethnic attribute continuously borrow.

---

[335] Yimamu, "Multi-cultural Accumulation", 101.

Epilogue

"Narratives play an important role in our lives. The stories we tell ourselves or those to which we listen shape our self-understanding and, hence, the ways in which we interact in our world."[336]

In their approximately 2000-year history, the five attributes of the identity of the Hunnic-Tlughish-Uyghurs have gone through a lengthy and complex process of transformation and change, in line with the ethnic group's glory and humiliation and the advance and decline of its civilization. These changes that resulted from religious or political forces deconstructed or diluted the identity of the Uyghurs in different historical periods and caused them to establish new identities. These new identities were used to cater or adapt to the prevailing religion or politics of the time, or for the simple need to upgrade their civilization.

Moreover, because of long being subjected to interference from the narratives of the Uyghurs themselves, as well as from the narratives of the Han-Chinese, of other Turkic language speaking peoples and Turkish people, and of the Mongols—narratives that stemmed from ethnic, political, religious, and ideological interests—this process included many misunderstandings and much confusion that have misled even academia. Therefore, the

---

[336] Rodney L. Petersen, *Preaching in the Last Days* (New York: Oxford University Press, 1993), 3.

thesis seeks to provide an alternative narrative on the historical Uyghur identity through intentional objective historical research.

The study of Central Asia-Xinjiang often triggers extra-academic passions and positions that are politically correct, religiously correct, or ethnocentric. In this thesis, I have not sought to curry favor with nor offend any community or ethnic group. Not to skirt the issue, this thesis was initially written in Chinese, so the viewpoints are from a Chinese perspective and the geographic orientation is that of the Xinjiang region. My only desire is to describe historical facts as accurately as possible and with scholarly conscientiousness, and to interpret them as objectively as possible, so as to advance the understanding of the historical Uyghur identity with an upgrade to narratives and assertions.

This thesis also seeks to advance academic exchange between Western and Asian scholars in this field, especially with regards to the results of research into Chinese historical materials. Some of the perplexing questions and elusive answers, micro or macro, that have long plagued the study of Central Asia can be clarified and resolved through deep and extensive digging into and more careful examination of the relevant Chinese historical texts, which have mostly been studied by other scholars through different frameworks and perspectives, or even alternate intentions.

(35,482)

www.ingramcontent.com/pod-product-compliance
Lightning Source LLC
Chambersburg PA
CBHW030221170426
43194CB00007BA/813